GREEN

# HBJ SCIENCE
— Nova Edition —

**Elizabeth K. Cooper**
formerly Coordinator
of Teacher Training
University of California

**Paul E. Blackwood**
formerly Specialist for
Science Education
U.S. Office of Education

**John A. Boeschen**
formerly Science Teacher
Pinole, California

**Morsley G. Giddings**
Professor of Education
Brooklyn College, City University
of New York

**Arthur A. Carin**
Professor of Elementary and
Early Childhood Education and
Director of Environmental Education
Queens College
City University of New York

*Biology and Ecology*
**Garrett Hardin**
Emeritus Professor of
Human Ecology
University of California
Santa Barbara, California

*Cooperative Learning*
**David W. Johnson**
Professor of Educational
Psychology
College of Education
University of Minnesota
Minneapolis, Minnesota

**Roger T. Johnson**
Professor of Curriculum
and Instruction
College of Education
University of Minnesota
Minneapolis, Minnesota

*Biology and Genetics*
**Richard C. Lewontin**
Professor, Harvard University
Cambridge, Massachusetts

*Geology and Earth Science*
**Alistair W. McCrone**
Professor of Geology
Humboldt State University
Arcata, California

*Physics*
**Franklin Miller, Jr.**
Emeritus Professor of Physics
Kenyon College
Gambier, Ohio

*Astronomy and Science Education*
**Fletcher G. Watson**
Emeritus Professor
Harvard University
Cambridge, Massachusetts

## Advisory Board

**Judy H. Dennison**
Coordinator of
Elementary Science
Fulton County Schools
Atlanta, Georgia

**Kathleen Donnellan**
Elementary Science
Resource Teacher
Springfield Public Schools
Springfield, Massachusetts

**Iris Maney**
Title II Staff
Development Specialist
Orleans Parish
New Orleans, Louisiana

**Dale Rose**
Supervisor of Science
Hampton School
Administration Center
Hampton, Virginia

**LaWanna S. White**
Science Supervisor
Cleveland Public Schools
Cleveland, Ohio

**HARCOURT BRACE JOVANOVICH, PUBLISHERS**
Orlando    San Diego    Chicago    Dallas

## Reviewers

Frances M. Culpepper
Instructional Services Center
Science Coordinator, K-12
Atlanta, Georgia

Robert W. Deem
Former Coordinator of Science,
    Health and Outdoor Education
School District 446
Elgin, Illinois

Marjorie Slavick Frank
Adjunct Faculty
School of Education
Manhattan College
Bronx, New York

Sister Anna Marie Goetz, R.S.M.
St. Maurice School
Pittsburgh, Pennsylvania

Deborah G. Gozzard
Science Teacher
Lynnhaven Junior High School
Virginia Beach, Virginia

Darlene Harmon
Clausell Elementary School
Jackson, Mississippi

Ernestine Hightower
Whittier Elementary School
Lawton, Oklahoma

Janet Iona
Adams County School District #12
Northglenn, Colorado

Patricia C. Manning
Professor, College of Education
University of Central Florida
Orlando, Florida

Thomasena Woods
Science Supervisor
Newport News Public Schools
Newport News, Virginia

PRINTED IN THE UNITED STATES OF AMERICA                    ISBN 0-15-364323-4

## PICTURE CREDITS

**Key:** (t) top, (b) bottom, (l) left, (r) right, (c) center.

**COVER:** Steinhart/Photo Researchers.

**Contents Pages: iii**(t), NASA, (c) George Holton/Photo Researchers, (b) Louise K. Broman; **iv**(t), Martin Bough/Corporate Studios Communications, (ct) Mike Mitchell/Photo Researchers, (cb) Zig Leszczynski/Animals, Animals, (b) Peter Miller/Photo Researchers.

**ILLUSTRATORS:** Craven Graphics, Mulvey Associates, Publisher's Graphics, Lloyd Birmingham.

**Unit 1:** Pages; **viii**(l), Pictor/DPI, (tr) Peter Beck/Photo Library, (br) Ginger Chih; **1**(tl, tr), NASA, (b) D. W. Funt/Art Resource, NY; **3, 4**(both), **5,** NASA; **6,** Dick Hufnagle/Monkmeyer; **8**(l), Ron Thomas/Alpha, FPG, (r) George H. Harrison/Grant Heilman; **9,** Bruce Moore/FPG; **11,** HBJ; **14**(l), Wide World Photos, (r) NASA; **15**(both), **16, 17**(both), **18, 20**(both), **21**(all), NASA; **22,** R. Hamilton Smith/Photo Library; **23**(both), **24,** NASA; **25,** Martin Bough/Corporate Studios Communications; **26**(t) NASA, (bl), Wide World Photos, (br) NASA/Wide World Photos; **27,** Wide World Photos; **28**(l), NASA, (r) Edith G. Haun/Stock, Boston; **29,** NASA; **30,** Douglas Kirkland/Contact Press Images/Woodfin Camp & Associates; **31,** NASA; **33,** UPI;

**Unit 2: 34**(l), Jeffry W. Myers/FPG, (tr), Ellis Herwig/Stock, Boston, (br) HBJ Photo; **35**(t), Jeffry W. Myers/FPG, (b) Eric L. Wheater/Image Bank; **36**(t), Karl & Steve Maslowski/Photo Researchers, (b) Mary M. Thatcher/Photo Researchers; **37**(t), Breck P. Kent/Animals,Animals, (c) Robert Rattner, (b) Hans Von Meiss Teuffen/Photo Researchers; **39**(l), Al Giddings/Bruce Coleman, (r) E. R. Degginger; **41**(tl), Tom Laughlin/Taurus, (tc) S. J. Krasseman/Peter Arnold, (tr) B. J. Ullman/Taurus, (b) E. R. Degginger; **42**(tl), Leonard Lee Rue/Photo Researchers, (tr) Karl Weidman/Earth Scenes, (bl) C. Allen Morgan/Peter Arnold, (br) Kenneth W. Fink/Photo Researchers; **43**(tl), Photo Researchers, (tr) George Holton/Photo Researchers, (bl) F.J. Dias/Photo Researchers, (br) William E. Townshend/Photo Researchers; **44,** Martin Bough/Corporate Studios Communications; **45**(t), F. Bauendam/Peter Arnold, (b) Runk, Schoenberger/Grant Heilman; **46**(tl), A. Power/Bruce Coleman, (tr) Gregory K. Scott/Photo Researchers, (bl, br) Zig Leszczynski/Animals, Animals; **47**(tr) John R, MacGregor/Peter Arnold, (cr) National Audubon Society/Photo Researchers, (clt), Stephen Dalton/Photo Researchers, (clb, b), Hans Pfletschinger/Peter Arnold; **48**(t, c), John R. MacGregor/Peter Arnold, (bl) R. Andrew Odum/Peter Arnold, (br) Russ Kinne/Photo Researchers; **49**(tl), John R. MacGregor/Peter Arnold, (tr) Peter B. Kaplan/Photo Researchers, (c) Tom McHugh, Steinhart Aquarium/Photo Researchers, (b) C. Allen Morgan/Peter Arnold; **50**(tl, tr), Hans Pfletschinger/Peter Arnold, (b) R. Andrew Odum/Peter Arnold; **51**(t), R. Andrew Odum/Peter Arnold, (b) Bruce Roberts/Photo Researchers; **52**(t), E. Hosking/Bruce Coleman, (c) Leonard Lee Rue III/Photo Researchers, (bl) Christa Armstrong/Rapho Div./Photo Researchers, (br) Jen & Des Bartlett/Bruce Coleman; **53**(t), C. Laubscher/Bruce Coleman, (b) J. L. Lepore/Photo Researchers; **54**(t), FPG, (c, bl) Jane Burton/Bruce Coleman, (br) Hans Reinhard/Bruce Coleman; **55**(tl), Bruce Coleman, (tr) Kojo Tanaka/Animals, Animals, (b) Juan & Carmecita Munuz/Photo Researchers; **56**(l, br), M. P. Kahl/Photo Researchers; (tr) Gregory K. Scott/Photo Researchers; **58**(both), Martin Bough/Corporate Studios Communications; **61**(l), Mark Boulrow, (r) Stephen Dalton/Photo Researchers; **62**(tl), Robert B. Evans, La Mer Bleu Productions/Peter Arnold, (tr) Zig Leszczynski/Animals, Animals, (b) Mark Antman/Image Works; **63**(tl, tr), Hans Pfletschinger/Peter Arnold, (b) Zig Leszczynski/Animals, Animals; **64**(l), Hans Pfletschinger/Peter Arnold, (r) Tom McHugh/Photo Researchers; **65**(both), Martin Bough/Corporate Studios Communications; **66**(t) Fred Bauendam/Photo Researchers, (bl), J H. Robinson/Photo Researchers, (br) Hans Pfletschinger/Peter Arnold; **67**(tl, bl), Hans Pfletschinger/Peter Arnold, (r) Jeffrey Sylvester/FPG; **68**(tl) Breck P. Kent, (tr), Bryan Hitchcock, (c) Eve Solum/Bruce Coleman, (b) P. W. Grace/Photo Researchers; **69,** Hans Pfletschinger/Peter Arnold; **70**(tl), J & C Kroeger/Animals, Animals, (tr) Tom McHugh/Photo Researchers, (b) Michael Heron/Woodfin Camp & Assoc.; **71**(t), Leonard Lee Rue III/Photo Reseachers, (c) John A. MacGregor/Peter Arnold, (bl) A. Power/Bruce Coleman, (bc) J. H. Robinson/Photo Researchers, (br) Robert B. Evans/Peter Arnold; **72**(t), Tom McHugh/Photo Researchers, (cl) D. K. Purse/Photo Researchers, (cr) Russ Kinne/Photo Researchers, (bl) George Holton/Photo Researchers, (bc) Sam Dasher/Photo Researchers, (br) Randy Matusow; **73,** Leonard Lee Rue III/Photo Researchers;

**Unit 3: 74**(l), Harvey Lloyd/Peter Arnold, (tr) Louise K. Broman/Photo Researchers, (br) Breck P. Kent/Earth Scenes; **75**(t), D. Lyons/Bruce Coleman, (b) E. R. Degginger; **76,** John Blaustein/Woodfin Camp & Assoc.; **77,** HBJ; **78**(both), Martin Bough/Corporate Studios Communications; **79**(tl, tr), Coco

*(continued on page 266)*

# Contents

## Planet Earth in Space     1

1. On a Spaceship to the Planets    2
2. A Stop on Earth    8
3. We Visit More Planets    14
4. The Real Journey into Space    20

## Animals of Planet Earth     35

1. Animals Are Alive    36
2. A Place to Live and Grow    39
3. Groups of Living Things    42
4. Animals with Backbones    57
5. Animals Without Backbones    61

## Plants of Planet Earth     75

1. Green—A Color for Plants    76
2. With Tubes and Without Tubes    80
3. With Seeds and Without Seeds    86
4. Without Chlorophyll    92

**4**

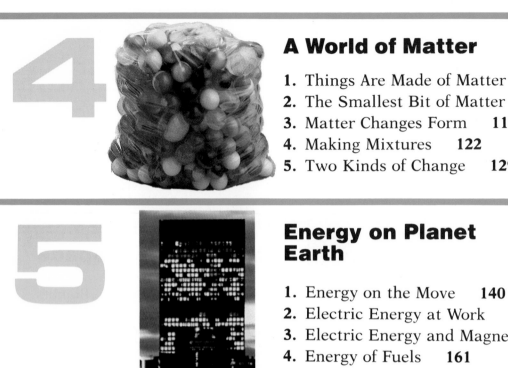

## A World of Matter  103

1. Things Are Made of Matter  104
2. The Smallest Bit of Matter  112
3. Matter Changes Form  118
4. Making Mixtures  122
5. Two Kinds of Change  129

**5**

## Energy on Planet Earth  139

1. Energy on the Move  140
2. Electric Energy at Work  147
3. Electric Energy and Magnets  152
4. Energy of Fuels  161
5. Coal, Petroleum, Natural Gas  166
6. Energy for the Future  174

**6**

## Fitness to Live  187

1. Fit to Find Food  188
2. Fit for Heat and Cold  196
3. Safe from Enemies  206
4. Fitness of Young Animals  214

**7**

## People on Planet Earth  225

1. People Live in Different Places  226
2. Using Your Brain  233
3. People Can Change Earth  242

**Glossary  256**
**Index  261**

GREEN

# HBJ —Nova⁜Edition— SCIENCE

# Planet Earth in Space

People can travel in many different ways. To get to a park for a picnic you might take a bus or a car. You could even walk! To visit someone far away you might have to go by train or plane.

Some people have made special trips into space. They are astronauts. Why were their trips special? How did they travel? What did they find when they were in space?

# 1 ▶ On a Spaceship to the Planets

Take an exciting journey right now. It won't be in a car or even a plane. You won't need a suitcase. You won't need a ticket. All you need is your imagination.

You are in a spaceship far out in space. In the distance you can see the Sun. It glows with a bright yellow light. Near the Sun are nine other bodies in space. These bodies are called **planets.** The planets move around the Sun. They spin like tops, too. The Sun and the planets make up our **solar system.** ■

Uranus

Jupiter

Sun

Each planet that you see is traveling around the Sun. Each travels in its own path called an **orbit.** Some planets travel fast. Others travel slowly. They take a long, long time to complete one orbit around the Sun. Our journey starts now. Our ship will travel through the solar system.

## First Stop—Mercury

We pass by Mercury. 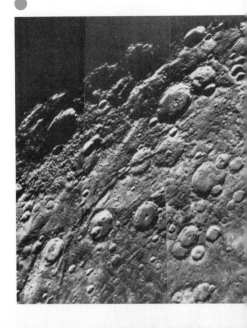 It is a small planet. It is the planet closest to the Sun. Mercury is so hot we cannot land. A day on Mercury is much hotter than the hottest day on Earth.

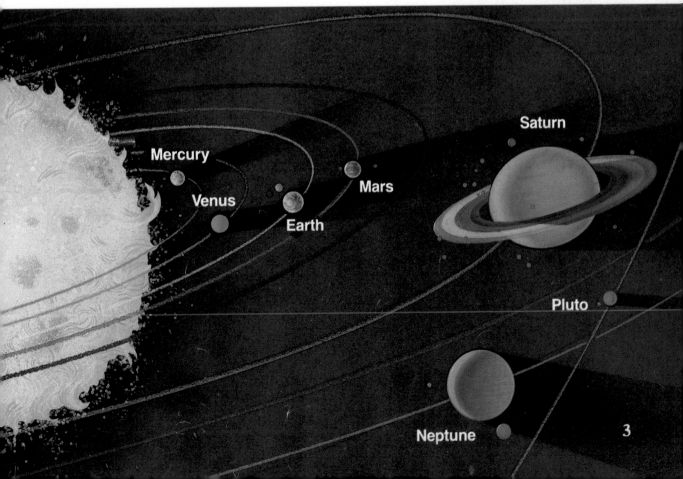

Mercury

Venus

Earth

Mars

Saturn

Pluto

Neptune

3

You see only dry valleys and mountains. There are no plants or animals here. None of the living things we know could live in such heat. We don't want to stay here very long.

## A Bright Spot—Venus

Ahead of us we see a bright spot in space. ■ People on Earth can see it, too. They call it the "Evening Star." Yet it is not a star at all. It is another planet—Venus.

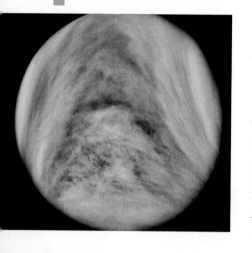

Thick clouds cover Venus. It is hard to see what the planet is really like. So let's take a closer look. Venus is about as big as Earth. It has mountains and plains like Earth. This huge canyon on Venus is much bigger than our Grand Canyon. ●

▲

Venus is different from Earth in many ways. It is very, very hot on Venus. There is no water to be seen. Can plants or animals live here? No. This planet is too hot and dry. Let's go on.

## The Third Planet—Earth

The next stop is the third planet from the Sun. It looks like a blue and white marble. Let's get closer. ▲

Now you can see more clearly. The blue color is water. The white is a patch of fluffy clouds. Fly around the planet. What do you

see? ■ The land is green with plants. There are animals in the air. There are animals in the water. On land, animals crawl, hop, walk, run.

There are people on this planet. They work and play. They think and learn. They talk. They write. They paint. They make music. They do amazing things.

Of course, you have been here before. This is your planet, Earth. Earth is not too hot. It is not too cold. It is just the right distance from the Sun. Earth is just right for us. It is right for the plants and animals that share the Earth with us.

Write each sentence with the best ending.

1. Our solar system has
   eight planets      nine planets      ten planets

2. Planets in our solar system travel around
   the Earth      the Sun      the Moon

3. Each planet has its own
   Sun      plants      orbit

4. The planet nearest the Sun is
   Earth      Mercury      Venus

5. To see plants and animals, visit the planet
   Mercury      Earth      Venus

## YOU CAN DISCOVER

Look at the space map on pages 2 and 3. Make one of your own. Will you use paper and crayons? Or will you build one? ●

# 2 ▶ A Stop on Earth

Your spaceship lands on Planet Earth.
You land on a hill near a waterfall. ■
There are tall trees and many other plants.
There are insects, birds, and other animals. ●

■

No other planet has these living things.
As far as we know, no other planet has large
bodies of water either. Almost three fourths
of Earth is covered with water.

## Energy Reaches Earth

Imagine that you have landed near the
equator. The air is very warm. In fact, this
part of the Earth is warm all year round.

Suppose you had landed near the South Pole instead. You would have found a land of ice and snow. ▲   The South Pole is a part of Earth that is cold all the year.

The energy from the Sun—**solar energy**—reaches all the Earth. From solar energy the Earth gets light and heat. Why then is one part of the Earth always cold? Why is another part always warm?

Look at a model of the Earth and the Sun. ◆   Follow the rays of light from the Sun that reach the Earth. At the equator the rays hit the Earth almost directly. Here the Earth gets plenty of solar energy. It is warm.

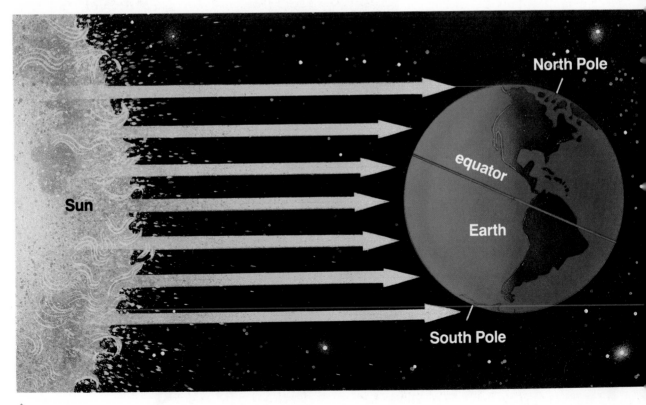

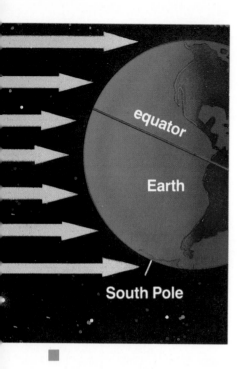

equator

Earth

South Pole

Look what happens at the South Pole. ■ The rays hit the Earth at a slant. The solar energy is spread thinly over this part of the Earth. This is why it is cold there.

## Earth Traps Heat

The Earth is like a thermometer inside a jar. There is a layer of air around the Earth. Solar energy that hits the Earth turns to heat. The Earth is warmed. The air around the Earth gets warm, too. ● The air traps the heat. *ACTIVITY*

## Make a Heat Trap

**You can use:** 2 pie tins, 2 thermometers, clay, a glass jar, sunlight

1. Put the pie tins in a sunny window. Put a lump of clay in each tin. Stand the thermometers in the clay. Don't let the clay cover the bulbs of the thermometers.

2. Wait until the thermometers reach the same temperature. Then put a glass jar over one of the thermometers. The jar has air in it. When the jar is upside down, the air is trapped inside.

3. Which thermometer gets warmer? ▇ Why?

What happens when the Sun doesn't warm the Earth? What happens to the heat at night?

The Earth is always turning. As it turns, one side faces the Sun. That side has day. The other side is in shadow. That side has night. ■

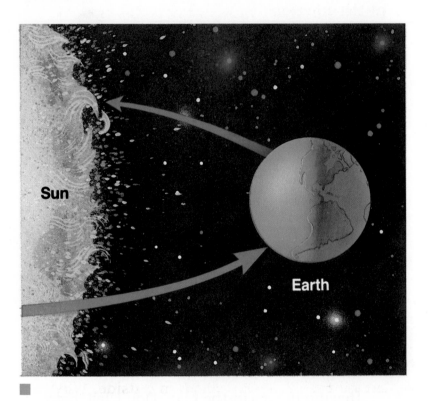

Sun

Earth

The night side of the Earth cools off. A little of the Earth's heat leaks away. It goes into space. Most of the heat is held though. The layer of air around the Earth holds the heat of the Sun.

The air traps the heat. What do you think Earth would be like if it had no way to hold heat?

Write each sentence with the best ending.

**1.** Solar energy that hits the Earth becomes
   rain    heat    sound

**2.** Solar energy is spread thinly
   at the South Pole    all over the Earth
   at the equator

**3.** The Earth's air traps
   sound    light    heat

**4.** The half of the Earth in shadow at night
   cools off    heats up    freezes everywhere

**5.** The Earth would be colder at night without
   air    plants    animals

## YOU CAN DISCOVER

**1.** The Earth's blanket of air traps heat of the
   Sun. Do other planets have blankets of air?

**2.** A greenhouse is made of glass. ● Inside the
   greenhouse it is warmer than outside. Why?

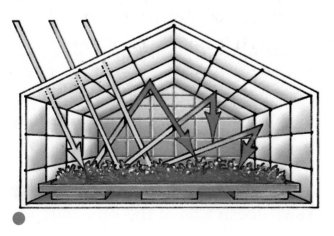

Earth is a beautiful planet. Even so, we must continue our journey. There are still many wonderful things to see.

From Earth we take off for the "Red Planet." ■ Can you see why Mars is called that name?

## **Mars and Earth**

Mars has soil—red soil. ● The soil has iron in it. We have iron on Earth, don't we?

Earth and Mars are alike in another way. They both have moons. Earth has one moon. Mars has two small moons. ▲

Remember how Earth looked from space? Mars doesn't have the blue patches of water. Yet it does have some ice—solid water. The ice forms "caps" like the North and South Poles of Earth.

It is day on Mars right now. It feels like a spring day on Earth. We must leave before night though. A night on Mars is very, very cold. The air on Mars is different from the air on Earth. It is thinner. It traps less heat. Mars cools off quickly at night.

Day and night on Mars are about as long as they are on Earth. But a year has about 700 days. It takes Mars almost two of our years to make one trip around the Sun.

## The Big Red Spot—Jupiter

Our next visit takes us to the largest planet—Jupiter. ◆ Imagine this. Jupiter is so big that 1,400 Earths could fit inside!

What a strange planet this is. We see only clouds. The clouds are always moving. A Giant Red Spot also moves and changes in the clouds. It never goes away. No one knows just what the spot is.

We can see many moons that travel around Jupiter. ■ You can count at least 16. There is also something we have not seen before. Jupiter has a ring around it. The ring is made of small particles.

It takes Jupiter about 12 years to travel once around the Sun.

■

## Rings Inside Rings—Saturn

Perhaps our next stop will be your favorite. This is the planet Saturn. Beautiful, isn't it? ● It is so different from other planets we have seen. Saturn has many bright rings around it. There are rings inside rings. ▲ Like the ring around Jupiter, these rings are made of small particles, too. Also traveling around Saturn are 23 moons.

Saturn is a very cold planet. It may be colder than Jupiter.

It takes Saturn 29 years to travel once around the Sun.

▲

## Uranus, Neptune, and Pluto

The last three planets are far, far away from the Sun. Imagine just how cold they must be!

Like Saturn, the planet Uranus has rings around it. ■ It has 15 moons, too.

Neptune is even colder than Uranus. ● It takes about 165 years for one trip around the Sun. Neptune has 2 moons.

Pluto is the farthest from the Sun. ● It is the coldest planet. It takes the longest to go around the Sun—about 248 years.

Pluto is our last stop on this imaginary journey. Is it the last planet? We don't really know. Perhaps someday other planets will be found.

Write each sentence with the best ending.

1. The soil of Mars has
   iron     plants     bugs

2. Nights on Mars are
   warm     very cold     like spring

3. The planet farthest from the Sun is
   Pluto     Saturn     Neptune

4. The orbit of each planet around the Sun takes
   the same time     a different time     one day

5. The planet with many bright rings is
   Neptune     Saturn     Pluto

## YOU CAN DISCOVER

Imagine yourself on a trip to a planet. ▲
What will you bring on your trip? What will you
find when you get there? Write a story about
your trip. Or draw pictures that tell a story.

19

# 4 ▶ The Real Journey into Space

You have taken a journey in your imagination. The things you have seen, though, are real. What you have learned about the planets is real. How can you know about planets that are so far away?

## Spacecraft Study the Planets

Spacecraft like these have traveled to the planets. ■ Some have landed. Some flew past. They all sent information back to Earth.

A spacecraft called Viking landed on Mars. A long arm reached out to scoop up some of the red soil. ● Viking found some water in the soil. But it did not find any living things on Mars.

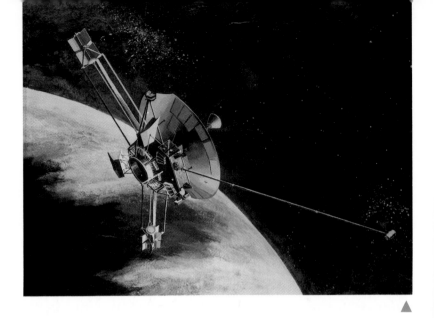

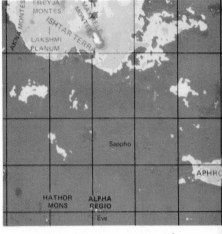

A spacecraft called Pioneer sent back photographs of Venus. ▲   Before Pioneer, we did not know about the mountains on Venus. We did not know about the plains. Now we can make a map of Venus. ◆

The Voyager 2 spacecraft is on a long journey. So far, it has given us information about Jupiter, Saturn, and Uranus. It took this picture of the rings of Saturn. ★

The journey of Voyager 2 is not over. The spacecraft is going through the galaxy to Neptune and then maybe to Pluto.

What will we learn about our solar system? We have to wait and see.

## The Moon—Our Neighbor in Space

You don't have to go out in space to see a certain object in space. All you have to do is look outside on a clear night. ■ You will see the Moon of Earth.

The Moon is Earth's **satellite.** It is in orbit around the Earth. ● It makes one trip around the Earth in about 4 weeks.

Sun

Earth

Moon

Why do you see the Moon at night? At night you are on the dark side of the Earth. Yet the Moon is in sunlight. The Moon gets its light from the Sun.

## The Face of the Moon

If you could look at the Moon through a telescope, this is what you would see. ▲ You would see flat places and high places. You would see deep holes called **craters.** ◆ The craters were made by space material hitting the Moon.

With telescopes, scientists have studied the Moon. They saw that the Moon always keeps the same side toward the Earth.

We always see the same side of the Moon. The Moon *turns*. As it turns the same side always faces the Earth. ACTIVITY

We do know what the other side looks like. We sent a spacecraft around the Moon. It took pictures of the other side. The other side of the Moon is the same as the side we always see! ■

■

## Visitors on the Moon

The Moon is 400 thousand kilometers from Earth. Yet it is our nearest neighbor in space. So it was the first place that we visited. On July 20, 1969, astronauts Edwin Aldrin and Neil Armstrong landed on the Moon. They wore space suits. They carried oxygen to breathe.

## How We See the Moon

**You can use:** signs for *Earth, Moon,* and *Sun,* and two friends to help

**1** You will be the Moon. Ask a friend to be the Sun. Ask another friend to be the Earth.

**2** The Moon should stand near the Earth. The Sun should stand farther away.

**3** Move in a circle around the Earth. Be sure you always face the Earth. ■

**4** Ask the Earth, "How many sides of the Moon do you see?" Tell the Sun, "Watch me as I go around the Earth. Do I *turn* as I go around the Earth?"

They had a television camera. ■ People all over the world saw pictures of the Moon.

Other astronauts have taken the same journey. Some explored the Moon with a car they called Moon Rover. ● They collected samples of rock and sand. ▲ Many scientists have studied the samples. They did not find any signs of water, of air, or life on the Moon.

## Journeys of the Future

We have made machines to travel in space. They have landed on the Moon. They have flown past planets.

We have built other machines. They have taken astronauts into space.

These machines are space stations. ◆ Perhaps one day people will live and work in them. One of those people could be *you*. Just imagine what that will be like!

# EXPLORING SCIENCE AND TECHNOLOGY

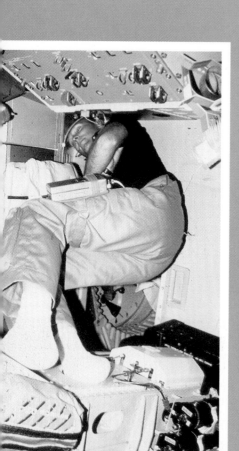

## Computers at Work

Out in space, the astronauts are asleep. ■ Will their spacecraft still run safely? Yes! A machine is at work. The machine is a computer.

People use computers to help them solve problems. ● Computers are tools. They are technology tools. *Technology* (tehk NAHL uh jee) is the use of tools or materials, or a certain way of doing things that helps people.

There are computers at many supermarkets. What do these computers do?

If you look at any box in your grocery cart, you may see a set of lines and numbers. They are a kind of code. At the check-out counter, a special light "reads" the code. Then the computer knows what each item is and how much it costs. It adds up the prices so you know how much to pay.

Write each sentence with the best ending.

1. We get information about the planets from
   stars    spacecraft    the Moon

2. The Earth's satellite is
   the Sun    Mercury    the Moon

3. The Moon gets its light from the
   Sun    Earth    other planets

4. When we look at the Moon, we always see
   a different side    the same side    all its sides

5. As the Moon goes around the Earth, it
   does not turn    turns    makes light

## YOU CAN DISCOVER

1. Many planets have satellites, or moons. Find out which ones they are. Do some planets have more than one moon?

   One moon of Jupiter is called Io. ■ It is a very special moon. See if you can find out why.

2. A special kind of spacecraft is being used to explore the solar system. It is called a space probe. Find out how space probes are different from other spacecraft.

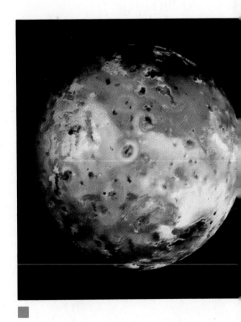

## Learning to Think Like a Scientist

An astronomer (uh-STRAHN-uh-mur) is a person who studies objects in space. Astronomers use telescopes to study the planets, the moon, and other parts of the solar system. ■ They study photos that are sent back to Earth to learn more about the objects in space.

Everyone with an interest in space can be an amateur astronomer. You can use binoculars or a telescope to study the sky. ● On a clear night, when there is no moon, you can see the stars. Maybe, you will see something in the sky that no one has ever seen before. When an astronomer sees something in the sky, he or she checks to make sure the object is really in the sky. The astronomer keeps looking and studying the sky. You can do the same thing as you learn to think like a scientist.

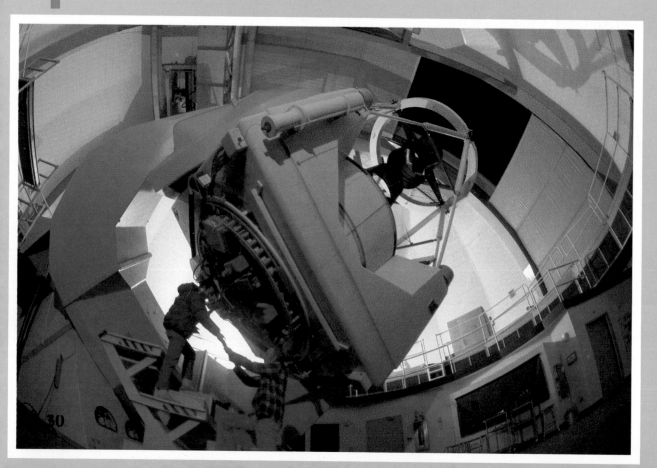

✓ Nine planets are in orbit around the Sun. Planet Earth is one of them.

✓ Moons travel around some of the planets. Planet Earth has one moon.

✓ We call the planets and their moons and the Sun the solar system.

✓ Energy from the Sun travels through space. The planets and moons nearer the Sun get more energy. Those farther from the Sun get less.

✓ Planet Earth gets light and heat from the Sun's energy. It is the right amount for our living things.

✓ We get information about the solar system from the journeys of spacecraft.

✓ The main idea of this unit is:

**Planets and moons of the solar system get energy from the Sun.**

## A. USE THE PICTURE TO ANSWER THESE QUESTIONS. ■

1.  Which planets get energy from the Sun?

2.  Which planets get more energy from the Sun than the Earth gets? Why?

3.  Which is the coldest planet? What makes you think so?

4.  Which planet takes longest to go around the Sun? Why?

5.  Which is the smallest planet? The largest?

1. Which planet is the right distance from the Sun? Why do you say so?

2. Why is the Sun an important part of the solar system?

3. How do we get information about the planets? What kind of information do we get?

# Find Out More

How many stars can you see on a clear night? You can't begin to count them!

Did you know that the Sun is a star, too? It is so bright that we can see it in the daytime. Just what is a star? How is it different from a planet?

# Challenge Your Thinking

The squirrel monkey's name is Miss Baker. ● Miss Baker was sent into space before any of the astronauts. Why?

●

33

# Animals of Planet Earth

You can find all sorts of things to eat at a supermarket. But you don't expect to find mustard with cereal. You don't find bananas with chicken. Each kind of food is easy to find. Why? The foods are in groups. Fruit is in one group. Meat is in another group. Grouping makes it easier to find what you need.

We can put living things in groups, too. We can put animals in groups. When the same kinds of animals are in a group it is easier to study them. Let's find out how.

A snowy owl builds a nest on the hard, rocky ground. The owl puts soft feathers in the nest. It puts in some moss plants.

The female owl lays eggs in the nest. After about 30 days, the eggs hatch. ■ The male owl finds food for the young birds.

Through the grass the elephants go. ● Big and small, they go. A mother watches over her baby. Her milk is food for the baby.

When the baby is older, it will get its own food. It will eat grass and leaves. It may eat fruit or sugar cane.

You know that the owl and the elephant are alive. How do you know?

## Living Things Reproduce

An owl grows. It lays eggs. Young birds hatch from the eggs. An elephant grows. It gives birth to live young. Animals make more animals, don't they? Animals can **reproduce.**

Plants grow. They make seeds. Young plants grow from the seeds. Plants can reproduce.

Animals need food to stay alive. ▲  They need water. ◆    They need air.

Plants need things to stay alive. They need food and water and air.

Do rocks need food? Do they need water or air? No. Rocks do not need these things. Rocks do not grow. They do not reproduce. That's how you know they are not alive.

37

Look at this picture. ■ Find things in the picture that are alive. Find things that are not alive.

■

## YOU CAN DISCOVER

Look around you. Find things that are alive. Find things that are not alive. Make a list. ● Now, here is a tricky question. Do you see anything that came from a living thing?

●

| Alive | Not Alive | Came from a Living Thing |
|-------|-----------|--------------------------|
| plant | plastic ruler | wooden desk |

A baby walrus has a lot of growing to do. It will grow to be as big as its parents. ▲

When it is very small, the walrus drinks milk from its mother. When it is old enough, it looks for its own food. A meal of clams is its favorite.

A walrus lives in the icy cold ocean. From the ocean, the walrus gets its food. The walrus depends on its surroundings, its **environment.**

A walrus must have the right environment to live. It needs a place where it can find food. All animals need food. ◆    All animals need a place where they can find food.

▲                                   ◆

## Getting Food

There are many plants and animals in this desert environment. ■ Each of them must have food or it cannot live.

The hawk eats a snake. The snake eats a mouse. The mouse eats the seeds and leaves of plants. Where does a plant get food?

A plant makes its own food. In sunlight, a plant makes food from soil, air, and water. A plant gets food from its environment. All living things get food from their environment.

**40**

Look at these pictures. ● Then answer the questions.

1. Which things depend on their environment?

2. Which do not depend on their environment?

3. Which ones are living things?

●

## YOU CAN DISCOVER

Discover an animal in your environment. ▲ Does the animal get its own food? Does it depend on people for food? Tell the class about the animal you discover.

▲

**41**

# 3 ▶ Groups of Living Things

Imagine being a space traveler. You have come to Planet Earth to study its living things. ■ There are so many! Each one seems so different from the next. How can you begin to learn about them all?

You can divide all living things into groups. Then you can learn about each group. You can put plants into one group. You can put animals into another group. Now let's learn about the animal group.

To make it easier, though, you can put the animals into smaller groups. These groups are called **classes.** Put animals that are alike into the same class. *ACTIVITY*

## Grouping

**You can use:** 10 different objects

**1** Get ten different things. They can be from home or from the classroom.

**2** Put all the things into two or three groups. Which things will you put together? All the things that have the same color? Shape? Size? Maria said she needed three groups for the objects she chose. Here are the groups she made. ■

**3** Now look at the living things on pages 42 and 43. How will you group them? What two groups could you use?

# Fish

What animal lives in ponds and lakes, in mountain streams, and in salty oceans? ■ In water everywhere, there are **fish.** Fish use their fins and tails to steer themselves through the water. Some fish have scales. ● Scales help protect a fish. With slippery scales, a fish can glide through the water easily.

■

Because a fish has gills, it can breathe under water. Have you ever seen a fish breathe? It takes in water through its mouth. It pumps the water over its gills. The gills take air from the water. The water is sent out through slits behind the head.

Most fish lay eggs. Young fish hatch from the eggs. The tiny new fish feed themselves.

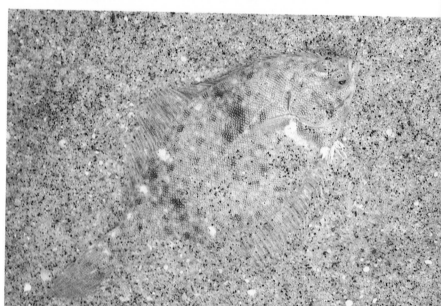

A lion fish lives in the Pacific Ocean. ■
Its home is a coral reef. This bass lives in a
lake. ●

A river in Africa might be the home of
these tiny neons. ▲  They can also live in
an aquarium.

Can you find the flounder? ◆  Its color
helps it to blend in with the ocean bottom.
Why do all these different animals belong in
the same class?

## Amphibians

This frog and this salamander are **amphibians.** ★ In a way, these amphibians have two lives. They hatch from eggs. The eggs are in the water. The young live in the water. They breathe with gills—like fish. They swim around, of course. This is the first part of their life.

★

As they grow, they change. ☐ They grow legs. Their gills disappear. They leave the water. They breathe with lungs. They can live on land. The second part of their life begins.

★

☐

Amphibians can live on land. They are never far from water though. They go back to the water to lay their eggs.

In the spring there may be many young frogs in a pond. The young frogs are called tadpoles. The adult frogs may be nearby, too.

You might see grass frogs. ■ They are very common. Or you might come across a big bullfrog. ● Look for this tiny frog in a tree. ▲

A pond or a stream is a good place to find this salamander. ◆ Look for it under a pile of wet leaves. Its bright yellow spots will help you find it.

★

★

## Reptiles

The turtle and the alligator are in the **reptile** class. ★ Snakes and lizards are, too.

A reptile's body is covered with scales or with plates. A turtle is covered with plates. So is an alligator. Look closely to see the scales on the snake. ☐ Lizards have scales, too. ○

☐

A fish with scales feels slippery. Reptiles with scales or plates aren't slippery. They feel dry to the touch.

Reptiles breathe with lungs. Some spend most of their time in water. They can't stay under water for very long though. They must come up for air.

○

49

Most reptiles reproduce by laying eggs.
They lay their eggs on land. ■ The shells of
the eggs are like leather. Most young reptiles
are on their own from the time they hatch. ●

In almost every kind of environment
there are reptiles. This lizard lives in the
desert. ▲ It is very colorful—and it is
poisonous! This king snake lives in the
desert, too. ◆

Is that a log floating in the swamp? ★
No, it's an alligator, waiting for a meal. The
alligator will eat crabs, fish, turtles, and
small animals. In fact, an alligator will eat
almost anything.

◆

★

## Birds

Have you seen a cardinal? ■ Can you recognize a chickadee? ● You probably know many kinds of **birds.**

Birds are alike in many ways. They all breathe with lungs. They have two legs and two wings. They all have feathers. They all lay eggs with hard shells.

Birds are also different in some ways. For one thing, not all birds can fly. Look at the ostrich. ▲ The ostrich is a tall bird on long, thin legs. Yet the ostrich has small wings. It can't quite get off the ground.

The loon is a water bird. ◆ Not only does it fly, but it is a good swimmer.

Some small birds, like sparrows, eat seeds. There are many kinds of sparrows. You can probably see them near your home. You may want to make feeders and houses for birds. ★ What kinds of birds come to the feeders? Some birds may make their nests in the houses you build for them.

This woodpecker is looking for food. ▫ It makes a hole in a tree to find ants or beetles. Its long, sticky tongue darts out. The food is caught!

The puffin lives in the cold North. ◉ To find its food, the puffin dives into the water. When its beak is full of fish, it goes back on land.

## Mammals

Most of the animals you know are **mammals.** Dogs and cats, pigs and rabbits are mammals. ■

Camels are mammals. ● Monkeys are, too. ▲ This may come as a surprise to you. Seals are mammals and so are whales. ◆

Did you think a whale was a fish? It may look like a fish. Yet that's not enough to put it in the fish class. A whale doesn't breathe like a fish. It doesn't lay eggs. In many ways whales are more like camels. Why are these animals mammals?

Mammals do not lay eggs. They give birth to live young. The young are fed milk made in the mother's body.

All mammals breathe with lungs. Even whales that live in the ocean have lungs. Whales can stay under water for a while. Then they have to come up to breathe.

All mammals have hair or fur. A rabbit has lots of fur. A whale has just a few hairs.

Write each sentence and fill in the best ending.

1. This animal has feathers and lays eggs.
   It is a _____ .

2. This animal has gills, fins, and a tail.
   It is a _____ .

3. This animal lives in the water and on land.
   It is an _____ .

4. This animal gives birth to live young.
   It is a _____ .

5. This animal has scales. It breathes with lungs.
   It is a _____ .

## YOU CAN DISCOVER

Some young animals are on their own from birth. Others are cared for by their parents. How do you think animals care for their young? ■ ■

Here are five animals. ● They belong in the five classes you studied. There is a fish, an amphibian, a reptile, a bird, and a mammal. These animals are alike in an important way. Each animal has a **skeleton.**

A skeleton is made of bones that help support the animal. Look at the red chain of bones in each skeleton. The chain of bones is called a **backbone.** *ACTIVITY*

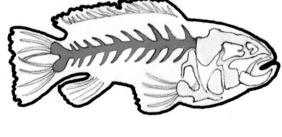

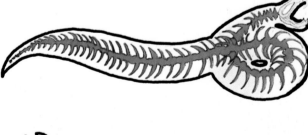

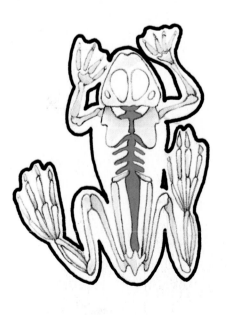

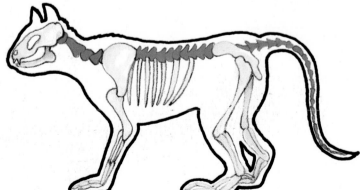

## What Does a Backbone Do?

**You can use:** 4 spools and a straw

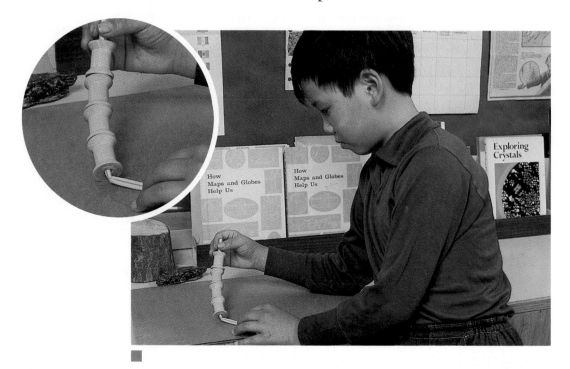

**1** Get a plastic straw and four empty spools of thread.

**2** Bend one end of the straw. Slide the spools on the straw. Then press the bottom spool against the table.

**3** Move the top spool over to one side a little. What happens? ■ Do you notice that each spool tilts a little? These little tilts add up. Then the chain of spools can bend a lot.

**4** Bend over. Can you feel the bones in your backbone? Now straighten up. What happens?

A backbone is made of many small bones. These bones are held together, yet they can move. Each small bone can move a little. The whole backbone can move a lot. A backbone helps an animal bend and move.

Feel the bones in the middle of your back. They are part of your backbone. What does your backbone help you to do?

## Inside the Backbone

Inside the backbone is the **nerve cord.** The nerve cord connects the brain to other parts of the body. ■ How does the nerve cord help an animal?

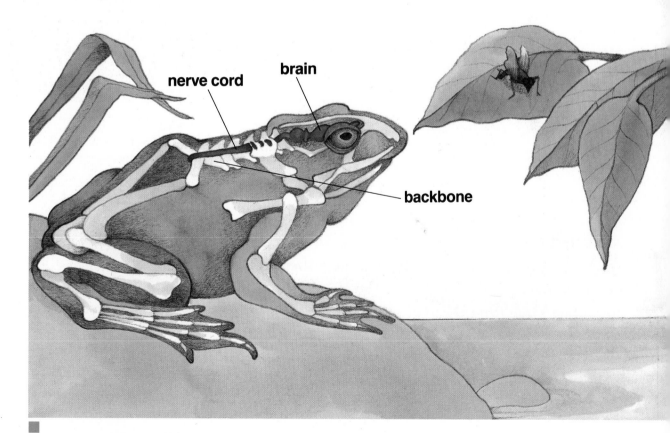

nerve cord

brain

backbone

It works this way. Suppose a frog sees a juicy fly. The brain sends a message. *Move closer to the fly.* This message travels down the nerve cord to the legs. Now the frog jumps to catch the fly and eat it!

## CHECK-UP TIME: Vocabulary . . . Facts . . . Concepts

Write each sentence with the best ending.

1. All animals in the five classes have
   backbones     feathers     scales

2. A backbone helps an animal
   bend and move     move fast only
   move slowly only

3. The backbone is made of
   large bones     small bones     one bone

4. Inside the backbone is the
   skeleton     brain     nerve cord

## YOU CAN DISCOVER

Would you like to put a backbone together? You could save the bones from a fish dinner. ■ Clean the bones of the backbone. Place them on a sheet of newspaper. Try to put the backbone together. How does the fish move?

With its long neck, the giraffe reaches up into the tree for food. ● The giraffe has a backbone. It helps the giraffe bend and move.

●

A mouse—much, much smaller than the giraffe—has a backbone, too. ▲ Most of the animals you know have backbones.

There are many kinds of animals without backbones. There are probably more than you can imagine. Here is how some of them are grouped.

▲

**61**

## Animals with Spiny Skins

In the sea live **animals with spiny skins.** They have no backbones. Most of these animals have rough skin with sharp spines.

Many of them are divided into five parts. You can see the five points of a starfish. ■ Look closely at the sea biscuit. ● Do you see five parts?

Most of these animals lay eggs.

## Mollusks

The sea is home for many **mollusks,** too. Mollusks have soft bodies. Most have hard shells they make themselves.

A clam has a two-part shell. ▲ To move around, the clam pushes a foot out of its shell. The muscles in the foot help to pull the clam along.

Snails are mollusks. Some snails live in salt water. Some live in fresh water. Some live on land. ◆ A snail moves very slowly. It can't run away from an enemy. So it gets inside its shell. ★ A snail makes a one-part shell.

The octopus has a soft body. ☐ It has no shell. It can squirt a kind of ink at its enemies. It can also change color and hide. How else is the octopus different from other mollusks?

◆

★

☐

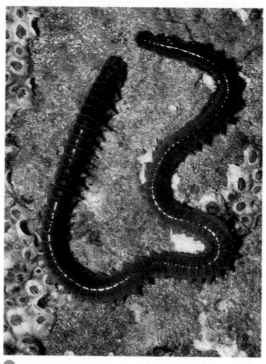

## Ringed Worms

Some animals have long soft bodies made up of sections, called rings. These **ringed worms** live on land and in water.

The earthworm lives on land. ■ The sandworm lives in water. ● They both have bodies made of many rings. They both lay eggs.

Watch an earthworm move. Its rings stretch out. Then they come together again.

An earthworm moves through the soil to find its food. The holes that an earthworm makes let air and water into the soil. The soil will be good for growing things. *ACTIVITY*

## The Work of an Earthworm

**You can use:** some earthworms, large jar, dark soil, sand, black paper

1. You can find earthworms. Just dig up some soil. After a heavy rain, you may even see earthworms on the surface.

2. Make a new garden for the earthworms. Put a layer of dark soil in the jar. Then put a layer of sand over it. Now add another layer of soil. ■

3. Put two or three earthworms in the jar. Wrap the jar in dark paper.

4. In a few days, look under the paper. ● What do you see? Can you see the trails the earthworms make? Have the soil and sand started to mix?

## Animals with Jointed Legs

Some of these animals live in the ocean. Some live on land. How then are lobsters, bees, and grasshoppers alike? ■

All these animals belong in the same group. They are **animals with jointed legs.** They all have legs that bend at the joints. Their skeletons are outside their skin. They reproduce by laying eggs.

**Insects** are the biggest class of animals with jointed legs. Some live on land, some live in fresh water. An adult insect has six legs and two feelers. Its body has three parts. An ant is an insect. ● A fly is, too. ▲ Is a spider an insect? ◆ Before you answer, count its legs!

# EXPLORING SCIENCE AND TECHNOLOGY

## Different-Colored Lobsters

Have you ever seen a lobster? Did you know that most lobsters are brown? Only one in 30 million is a different color.

A scientist in New York planned to raise different-colored lobsters. ■ He wanted to study how they move from one place to another.

Instead, he found that blue lobsters grow much faster than brown lobsters. ● Blue lobsters weigh one pound in just 20 months. It takes a brown lobster 5 to 7 years to weigh a pound. That's why lobsters cost so much money!

Scientists are using technology to raise blue lobsters. Also, they are trying to learn what makes blue lobsters grow so quickly. Then, maybe, they can grow other lobsters faster. Once they are able to do these things, maybe lobsters won't cost so much money.

Use pages 45 to 67 to classify the following animals.

1. The oyster lays eggs. It lives in the sea. It has a soft body inside a hard shell.

2. The sand dollar lives in the sea. It has a rough, spiny skin.

3. The grasshopper has six jointed legs. Its body has three parts.

## YOU CAN DISCOVER

There is an insect in this picture. ■ Can you find it?

The insect is hiding from its enemies—from a bird or a lizard. Do you think the insect has a good disguise?

■

## Spending Days at the Zoo

Would you like to have lunch with a camel? If you were a zookeeper, it would be just another part of your job.

Zookeepers help zoo animals stay healthy. They feed animals. They observe animals. They find out if any animals are sick or hurt. They wash cages and keep animals clean. It looks like fun—but it's hard work, too.

Zookeepers learn about animals. They learn what animals need to stay healthy.

✔ We can put things that are alike into groups. Scientists call this classifying. We classify things as alive or not alive.

✔ A living thing depends on its environment. It can reproduce.

✔ We classify things as plants or animals.

✔ We classify animals. We put animals that have backbones into one group. We put animals without backbones into different groups.

✔ We classify animals with backbones as fish, amphibian, reptile, bird, or mammal.

✔ The main idea of this unit is:

**Living things that are alike in some way can be put into a group.**

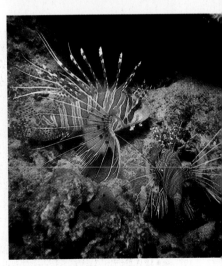

71

## A. USE THE PICTURES TO ANSWER THE QUESTIONS. ■

1. Which of these need food, water, and air?

2. Which ones grow?

3. Which can move around by themselves?

4. Which can reproduce?

5. How would you classify the animals?

## B. ANSWER THESE QUESTIONS.

1. Why do we put animals into groups?

2. Name the classes of animals with backbones. What kinds of animals do not have backbones?

3. Tell the story of a young amphibian. What happens as it grows?

4. Tell the story of a pet. It can be yours. Or it can belong to a friend. Where does it live? What does it need to live?

## Find Out More

Some ants, remember, build nests. In the ground. In a tree. Under leaves.

Many other kinds of animals build homes. Find out what kind of home a bee makes. Or a spider. Or a raccoon. ●

## Challenge Your Thinking

This animal is a mammal. It flies, but it does not have feathers. It hangs upside down during the day. At night, it comes out to find food. Its name is the same as something you use to play baseball. What is this animal?

# Plants of Planet Earth

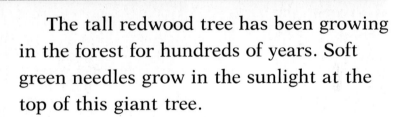

The tall redwood tree has been growing in the forest for hundreds of years. Soft green needles grow in the sunlight at the top of this giant tree.

On the forest floor, some plants are growing in the shade. The green leaves of fern plants look like lace. A bright green carpet is made of moss plants. Flowering plants also grow in the wet, shady places.

Thousands of kinds of plants live on Earth. How can we learn about these plants? Grouping makes it easier. Let's look at the plant kingdom.

The plants in the redwood forest are very different, aren't they? They are also quite different from the plants that grow in a hot, dry desert. ■ Yet in one way they are all alike. They are green. The plants in this greenhouse are green, too. ● In fact, most plants are green. Can anything change the color of a plant? ACTIVITY

## Do Plants Change Color?

**You can use:** radish seeds, soil, small box, container

**1** Plant radish seeds in a container of soil. Water the soil. The plants will grow quickly.

**2** After a few days, put a small box over half of the plants. Put the container in a sunny place.

**3** Wait three days. Then lift the box off the plants. ■ What do the covered plants look like? What do the uncovered plants look like?

■    ●

## Green Plants Make Food

In the sunlight, tiny radish plants grow tall and green. What happens to the plants in the dark? The plants lose their bright green color. They become pale and weak. If the pale plants stayed in the dark, they would die.

With sunlight, plants can make food. ■ The plants need air and water, too. They also need the green material. We call it **chlorophyll.** Without chlorophyll, the plants can't make food. ● Without it, they would die.

The green color, then, is important for plants. It helps plants do an important job.

Write each sentence with the best ending.

1. Most plants are alike because they are
   tall    short    green

2. Green plants are special. They make their own
   water    food    sunlight

3. To make food, plants need air, water, and
   a forest    shade    sunlight

4. The green coloring in plants is
   chlorophyll    moss    soil

## YOU CAN DISCOVER

Not all leaves are the same size or the same shape. Are they all the same color green? ▲ How can you find out?

# 2 ▶ With Tubes and Without Tubes

Did you ever change the color of flowers this way? ■ You put each white flower in a glass of water. Then you add different food colors to the water. What colors will you choose?

In a few hours, the flowers are no longer white. Each flower is a different color—the color of the water. ● The water with the food color has traveled to the top of the flowers. How does this happen?

## Plants with Tubes

Water travels through tubes in the stem of the flower. Most kinds of plants have tubes. Do you see the tubes in a piece of celery? ▲  The tubes carry water from the soil. The water can reach all parts of the plant.

There are tubes in corn plants. ◆  There are tubes in garden flowers and in grass stems. There are tubes in fern plants, too.

Remember the big redwood trees in the forest? Those trees have tubes. The tubes carry water all the way up to the needles at the very top. *ACTIVITY*

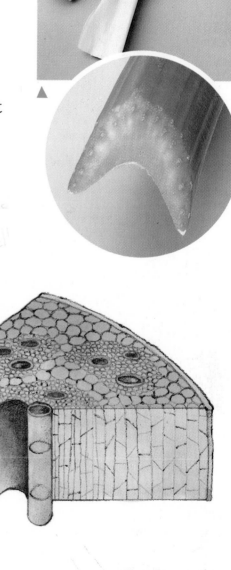

## Find the Tubes in Leaves

**You can use:** different kinds of leaves, white paper, crayons

**1** In a leaf, the tubes are called veins. The veins carry water. They also help give the leaf support. Look at the pattern of veins in different leaves. ■

**2** Make a print of the pattern. Here's how. Place a leaf face down. Put a piece of white paper over the leaf. Gently rub a crayon over the paper. ● Do you see a pattern of veins? ▲

**3** Make prints of other kinds of leaves. Do all the leaves have the same pattern?

## Plants Without Tubes

Some plants can grow very tall. They have tubes that carry water to all parts of the plant.

Other plants do not have tubes. They do not grow tall. They grow close to the ground—close to water. Moss plants do not have tubes. They never grow tall. ■ This drawing is bigger than a real moss plant. ● When many moss plants grow together, they look like a thick green carpet.

Moss plants have chlorophyll. They make their own food.

## Plants Helping People

Thousands of years ago, people used herbs and some plants to help them when they were sick. Today, doctors still use plants to help people get well.

With the help of modern technology, doctors are finding more plants to use as medicine. One such plant, called a rosy periwinkle, grows in tropical rain forests. ■ The rosy periwinkle is being used to help children who have leukemia.
*Leukemia* (loo KEE mee uh) is a serious disease of the blood. Before doctors found a way to use the rosy periwinkle, a child with leukemia had little chance of getting better. Now, the child's chances have improved.

Research is continuing so that doctors can find other plants like the rosy periwinkle. Someday, through the use of plants, maybe there will be a cure for all disease.

Write each sentence with the best ending.

1. Water moves to the top of a tree in
   flowers     tubes

2. Most kinds of green plants have
   tubes     no tubes

3. One kind of plant without tubes is a
   fern     moss

4. One kind of plant with tubes is
   moss     grass

5. Plants without tubes
   do not grow tall     grow very tall

## YOU CAN DISCOVER

This green algae grows in a pond. ■ It makes its food. It has no roots or stems or leaves. Do you think it has tubes?

■

On a summer day, you might like a slice of watermelon. ■ It's so cool and juicy. Yet all those seeds get in the way. Even though you may not like the seeds they are important. Let's see why.

These are watermelon vines. ● They have many flowers. A bee may fly from flower to flower. When the flowers die the fruit begins to grow. Small watermelons grow where the flowers were. ▲

The watermelons grow larger. ◆ They get ripe. Inside each watermelon are seeds. If you plant the seeds you will get more vines. More vines make more fruit. Do you see why seeds are important?

The flowers of a plant are important, too. Seeds are formed inside a flower. **ACTIVITY**

# How Are Seeds Made?

**You can use:** lily or gladiolus, hand lens

1. Pull off some of the petals of a large flower.

2. Use a hand lens to look at the parts of the flower.

3. Look at the stamen. The top of the stamen makes pollen. Touch the stamen. ■ Do you find pollen on your finger?

4. In the center of the flower is the pistil. Touch the top of the pistil. Does it feel sticky?

5. The bottom of the pistil is thick. ● Split this thick part open with your fingernail. Look for the rows of tiny beads called ovules. An ovule can grow into a seed.

A bee is getting food. It flies to a flower. The hairs of the bee's body can touch the **stamen** of the flower. A yellow powder from the stamen stays on the hairs. The yellow powder is **pollen.**

The bee flies to another flower. Some of the pollen it carries sticks to the **pistil** of this flower. The flower is **pollinated.**

Here's what happens inside the flower. ■ A tube grows from the pollen. The tube goes down into the pistil. At the bottom are rows of tiny beads, called **ovules.** The tube goes into one of the ovules. The ovule grows into a seed.

The pistil grows, too. It becomes a fruit. Inside the fruit are the seeds of the plant.

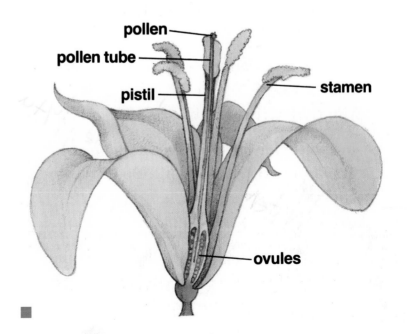

pollen

pollen tube

pistil

stamen

ovules

## Seeds Without Flowers

A peach tree has flowers and fruit. Inside the fruit are seeds. ●

A redwood tree does not have flowers. It does not have fruit. But it does have seeds.

A redwood tree has two kinds of **cones.** ▲ It has pollen cones. They have pollen. The redwood tree also has seed cones. They make seeds. Here's how.

Wind picks up pollen from pollen cones. Some of the pollen may reach the seed cones. The pollen reaches the ovules of the seed cones. The ovules grow into seeds. When the seeds are ripe, the seed cones open. The seeds fall out. The seeds may fall where they can live. Then new redwood trees will grow.

## Without Seeds

Ferns have roots, stems, and leaves. They have chlorophyll. So they make their own food. Ferns do not have flowers. They do not have seeds or fruit. How do new fern plants grow?

■

Do you see the brown spots on these fern leaves? ■ Each spot is full of brown powder. The powder is made of tiny **spores.** The spores fall out. Some land on damp soil. They can grow and make new fern plants.

Other plants make spores, too. Do you remember the tiny moss plant? It makes spores. Here is how the moss plant looks when it makes spores. ● These spores can make new moss plants.

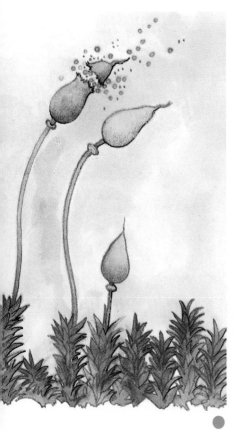

●

Write each sentence with the best ending.

1. Inside most fruits are
   seeds      flowers      cones

2. In a flower pollen grows a tube down into the
   pistil      stamen      seed

3. Inside a flower, an ovule can grow into a
   flower      cone      seed

4. A redwood tree has seeds. The seeds grow in
   flowers      cones      spores

5. A fern can grow from
   fruit      seeds      spores

## YOU CAN DISCOVER

Which are fruits?  ▲   How do you know?

▲

# Without Chlorophyll

You might find mushrooms growing on the forest floor. ■   Are they different from the plants in the forest? For one thing, they aren't green. They don't have chlorophyll.

■

A plant needs chlorophyll to make food. So mushrooms can't make their own food. What do they use for food?

■

Molds don't have chlorophyll either. You might find mold growing on bread or on fruit. ●   It even grows on wet shoes. What does mold use for food?

## Molds and Mushrooms Get Food

Mushrooms have no chlorophyll. Molds have no chlorophyll. They cannot make food.

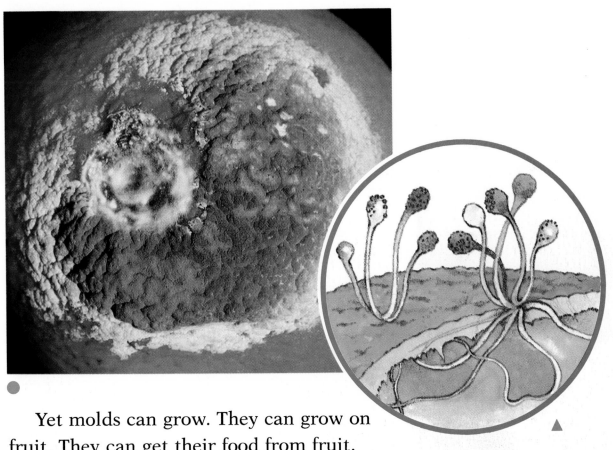

Yet molds can grow. They can grow on fruit. They can get their food from fruit. Here's how. Look at the mold through a hand lens. ▲ The mold has many tiny threads. Some of the tiny threads go right into the fruit. The mold takes its food from the fruit.

Molds that grow on fruit get food from the fruit. Molds that grow on bread get food from the bread.

Molds are **fungi.** Fungi are plants without chlorophyll. Mushrooms are fungi, too. Mushrooms that grow in the soil get food from the soil. Mushrooms that grow on a tree get food from the tree.

## Molds and Mushrooms Reproduce

Look at a mold again. ■ Do you see the tiny thread on top of the food? Many of the threads have balls on top. The ball is as big as the head of a pin. The ball has thousands of spores. When the ball breaks, out come the spores.

The spores are carried along in the air. Some may land on bread. Some may land on fruit or other food. These spores may grow into more molds. Molds reproduce from spores.

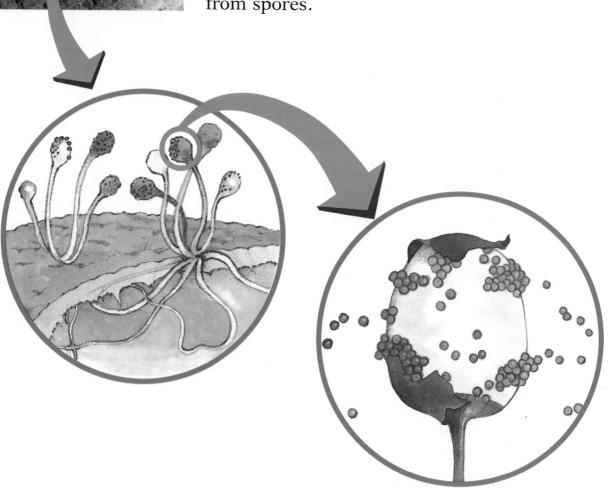

This is the way new mushrooms are formed. ● The threads of a mushroom are underground. Small buttons grow on the threads. A button grows upward. It gets bigger. The cap opens like an umbrella. There are thousands of spores inside the cap. The spores fall out.

Suppose the spores fall where they can live. Then they will become new mushrooms.

You can catch the spores of a mushroom. Then take a closer look at them. *ACTIVITY*

## Making a Spore Print

**You can use:** mushroom caps, white paper, bowl, hand lens

**1** Take the stem off a mushroom. Put the cap down on a piece of white paper.

**2** Cover the cap with a bowl. ■ On the next day, take the bowl away.

**3** Do you see the pattern of spores? ● You may want to use a hand lens to look more closely.

Write each sentence with the best ending.

1. To make food, a plant needs
   spores     fruit     chlorophyll

2. Fungi do not have
   chlorophyll     spores     threads

3. Fungi cannot make
   caps     spores     food

4. Molds can get food from
   fruit     spores     chlorophyll

5. Fungi reproduce from
   seeds     spores     eggs

## YOU CAN DISCOVER

Where does mold grow? ■ Does mold grow on bread in a refrigerator? On bread in a warm place? Does it grow on a dry cloth or a wet one?

■

97

**SCIENCE AND YOUR CAREER**

## Growing Better Plants

People are at work behind the glass walls. They are not in an office or a hospital. They are in a greenhouse. Green plants grow in the greenhouse.

These people know how plants grow. They pick the best seeds to grow the healthiest plants. They will sell some of the plants. They will use others to grow better plants. Some of the plants will have flowers with beautiful petals or flowers that smell sweet. Some will have better fruits and vegetables. Some will even have fruits without seeds.

Perhaps you will eat a seedless orange one of these people grew.

✓ Most plants are green. They have chlorophyll. They can make food.

✓ Most plants have tubes. Tubes help a plant get water. Some plants, like mosses, do not have tubes.

✓ Most green plants grow from seeds. Most plants with seeds have flowers. Some have cones. Seeds, flowers, and cones help plants reproduce.

✓ Molds and mushrooms do not have chlorophyll. They cannot make food. They get food from their environment. They reproduce from spores.

✓ Plants are living things. They grow and reproduce. They depend on materials in their environment.

✓ The main idea of this unit is:

**Plants that are alike in some ways can be put into groups.**

## A. CHOOSE THE BEST ANSWER.

1. A moss plant will never grow tall. It has no
   chlorophyll    tubes    leaves

2. The redwood tree grows tall. It has tubes. It
   makes seeds in
   cones    flowers    leaves

3. The fern has tubes. It does not make seeds. It
   can reproduce from
   tubes    cones    spores

4. An ovule of a flower can grow. It can make a
   petal    seed    leaf

5. A mushroom cannot make its own food
   because it does not have
   chlorophyll    tubes    leaves

## B. ANSWER THESE QUESTIONS.

1. How does water get to the top of a tall
   redwood tree?

2. How do fungi get food? How do they
   reproduce?

3. What happens when a flower is pollinated?
   Write a story. Or draw pictures.

## Find Out More

Yeast is a kind of fungi. It can't make its own food. It uses sugar for food. Try this with the help of an adult. Add 2 tablespoons of sugar to a cup of warm water. Then add a pinch of yeast. You can use the cake yeast or the powdered kind. Stir. What happens? ■ The yeast is growing! As it grows, it gives off bubbles.

To make some kinds of bread, you have to add yeast. What do the bubbles do to the bread?

■

## Challenge Your Thinking

Each of these seeds travels before it reaches the ground. ● Each travels in a different way. How do these seeds reach the ground? Use the pictures for clues.

# A World of Matter

A museum is an exciting place to visit. There may be toys from faraway places or clothes from long ago. There may be rocks and shells—even animals.

Look around you right now. Look around outdoors. You will find many interesting things. They are just as interesting as the things you can see in a museum. In fact, your whole world is a kind of museum. It is a museum you live in. All the things are made of matter. Let's find out about matter.

# 1 ▶ Things Are Made of Matter

Suppose you are picked for the school softball team. ■ You talk to your friends about it. You tell them:

"My uniform is red and white. I wear a hard blue cap. The bat is long and heavy. It is made of metal."

What else can you say about the things you use to play ball? You can describe the ball and the glove. When you tell what these things are like, you are describing **matter**. Matter is what all things are made of. ACTIVITY

## Describing Matter

**You can use:** 4 or 5 kinds of things, a sheet of paper

| Ball | Yarn | Cup | Pine Cone |
|------|------|------|-----------|
| round | soft | smooth | rough |
|  |  |  |  |
|  |  |  |  |
|  |  |  |  |
|  |  |  |  |
|  |  |  |  |
|  |  |  |  |

**1** Write the name of each thing on a sheet of paper.

**2** Look at the color of each thing. Look at the shape. Feel each one. ■

**3** List the words you use to describe each thing. ● Use words like *hard, soft, round, square, light, heavy, smooth, rough*. What other words do you need?

**4** Be sure to tell what color each thing is. Also tell what each is made of.

**5** Look at your lists. Are any two things exactly the same?

## Matter Takes Up Space

Look at the things on this page.  They are all different, aren't they? A book is not like a roller skate. A paper kite is not like a book or a skate. A sweater is not like an apple. Yet these things are alike in one way. They are all made of matter. All things are made of matter. Small and large, heavy and light—everything you can name is made of matter.

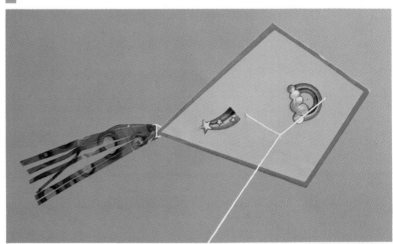

Matter takes up space. The jar is full of
oil. ● The oil takes up the space in the jar.
Can you add any more oil? The bag is full of
marbles. ● No more marbles will fit in the
bag. The marbles take up space in the bag.

Now pour the marbles out of the bag. ▲
Let's put something else in the bag. Blow
into the bag. ◆ The bag fills with air. Air
takes up space in the bag. Suppose you
want to make the bag flat again. What will
you have to push out?

## Matter in Three Forms

Marbles and oil and air are matter. They are three different forms of matter. Marbles are a **solid.** Wood is a solid. ■ This gate is made of iron. ● Iron is a solid.

The marbles have a shape. Their shape doesn't change. You can put the marbles in a bag. You can put them in a box. Marbles stay the same shape. The shape of a solid stays the same.

Oil is a **liquid.** So is water. Orange juice is a liquid, too. A liquid can change shape. Pour juice into a tall thin glass. ▲ Then pour it into a short wide bowl. ◆ Do you see how the shape of the liquid can change?

▲

◆

Most of the time you don't see the third form of matter. You know it's there though. Take a deep breath. You take air into your body. Air is a **gas.** A gas is a form of matter. Air fills these balloons. ★ It takes the shape of the balloons. A gas, such as air, changes shape.

## Finding Out About Matter

You can find out about matter by using your **senses.** Your senses are touch, hearing, taste, smell, and sight.

You can touch a brick wall. ☐ You can feel how rough it is. You can see its bright red color.

When you drink orange juice, you know it is not grapefruit or apple. The taste tells you. The smell and color tell you, too.

Air is a gas that you can't see or taste or smell. When air is moving, it makes a wind. You can feel the wind blowing. ■ You can see how the wind moves things. You can hear the leaves move when the wind blows through them.

You learn about matter with your senses. You learn about the world around you.

Write each sentence with the best ending.

**1.** All things are made of
air     gas     matter

**2.** A rock is matter. It is a
solid     liquid     gas

**3.** Milk is matter. It is a
solid     liquid     gas

**4.** Air is matter. It is a
solid     liquid     gas

**5.** You find out about matter by using
all your senses     only your eyes

## YOU CAN DISCOVER

How does a banana taste? Or a lemon?
Are they different? How? How else is a banana
different from a lemon? Use your other senses to
find out.

You don't have any trouble telling these things apart. ■ They look different. They feel different. Of course, they taste different. They even smell different.

## What Is Matter Made Of?

These foods—in fact, all things around you—are made of tiny particles. These particles are called **molecules.** A molecule is the smallest bit of something. Water is made of molecules. The smallest bit of water is a molecule of water.

Sugar is made of molecules, too. The smallest bit of sugar is a molecule of sugar.

Sugar and water are not made of the same kind of molecules. Different things are made of different kinds of molecules. Now you know why the foods are different. They are made of different molecules.

## A Molecule Hunt

Molecules are very, very tiny. A grain of sand is very small. A molecule is much smaller. One molecule alone is much too small to be seen.

Suppose you were the size of a molecule. Then a grain of sand might seem like a mountain to you. ●

Even though molecules are very small, you have ways of knowing that they are there. *ACTIVITY*

## Finding Molecules

**You can use:** a lemon, a glass, water, a straw

1 Taste the water in a glass. Use a straw. Taste water from the top of the glass. From the middle. From the bottom. Does the water have a sour taste?

2 Taste a drop of juice from the lemon. Sour, isn't it?

3 Now try this. Squeeze a few drops of lemon juice into the glass of water. Wait 10 minutes.

4 Now taste the water again. ■ Taste the water from the top. From the middle. From the bottom. How does the water taste now?

Suppose you add lemon juice to water. In a short time, all the water tastes sour, just like the lemon juice! Bits of the juice spread out in the water. These bits are molecules.

Even though you can't see the molecules, you know they are there. You can taste the lemon in the water. Suppose you add sugar to the water and stir. Then you taste the water. How do you know that there are molecules of sugar in the water?

## Using Your Sense of Smell

Ask your friends to close their eyes. Then open a bottle of vinegar. Molecules of vinegar go into the air. How do you know? You can smell the vinegar. Your nose is a molecule detector!

Do your friends know there is vinegar in the room? ■ How do they know? The molecules of vinegar spread out in the room. They mix with the molecules of air. Your friends smell the vinegar, too.

115

# EXPLORING SCIENCE AND TECHNOLOGY

## Listening for Molecules

It is midnight. Everyone in the house is asleep. Then a loud buzzing noise wakes them. The buzz is a warning. There is a fire in the building! ▪ The people leave at once.

What made the buzzing sound? It was a smoke detector. ● The smoke detector can find molecules in smoke. When the molecules reach the detector, the loud noise begins. The noise is a warning that a fire has started. After the people leave the building, they will call the Fire Department.

Do you have smoke detectors in your home or school?

Write each sentence with the best ending.

**1.** The smallest part of something is a
   molecule      grain

**2.** Molecules are
   very large      much too small to be seen

**3.** Different things are made of
   the same molecules      different molecules

**4.** Vinegar is left in a dish. The molecules will
   mix with molecules of air      change into water

## YOU CAN DISCOVER

Put a small amount of water in a glass. Add some sugar and stir. Look at the glass after a few days. ■ Which molecules have gone into the air? Which molecules stay behind?

Put a glass full of ice cubes in a sunny window. ■ After a while, the ice has melted. ● There is water in the glass.

■       ●

## Solid to Liquid

Ice is a solid. In a warm place it can become a liquid—water. Matter is changing its form. Heat can change a solid to a liquid.

You can change the form again. Put the water into a freezer. ▲ When the water gets cold enough, it will change to ice. A liquid can change to a solid.

When ice melts, no water is lost. No water is gained. When water freezes, no water is lost. No water is gained.

▲

## Liquid to Gas

After a rain, you see puddles on the sidewalk. ◆ What happens when the Sun comes out? The puddles slowly disappear. The water evaporates.

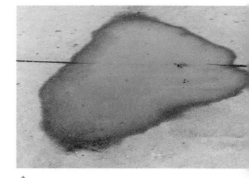

The water is changing form. It is changing from a liquid to a gas. The gas is called **water vapor.** The water vapor goes into the air. ★ You cannot see water vapor. It has no color.

When water changes to water vapor, no water is lost. No water is gained.

## Molecules Can Move

Imagine you can see molecules. In ice, molecules are close together. □ They can move back and forth. But they stay in the same place.

119

In water, the molecules can move. ■
They can slide over each other. They can
move more than the molecules of a solid.

There are molecules in water vapor. ●
Water vapor is a gas. Gas molecules move
more than any others. They can move in
any direction. One bumps into another.
They move off in different directions.

Write each sentence with the best ending.

**1.** Ice is a
   solid     liquid

**2.** When water turns to ice, it
   becomes a liquid     changes form

**3.** When water becomes a gas, its form
   changes     does not change

**4.** Water vapor is a
   liquid     gas

**5.** When water changes form,
   water is lost     water is not lost

## YOU CAN DISCOVER

Put some water in a plastic bag. Tie the bag tightly. Weigh the bag with the water in it. Put the bag in the freezer. The water changes to ice. Ice takes up more space in the bag. Does the ice *weigh* more than the water? ▲   Find out.

▲

# 4 ▶ **Making Mixtures**

Someone is chopping. Someone else is cutting. ■ Into the bowl go the carrots and celery. Cabbage and tomatoes go next. Mix them up. Add some dressing. The salad is ready. It's time for lunch!

Salad is a kind of **mixture,** isn't it? Lots of things are mixed together. ● Each is part of the salad. Yet each thing does not change. Carrots still have their orange color. Celery is still green. Tomatoes are still red. Each thing still tastes like itself, too. Mixing the foods does not change them. ACTIVITY

## Mixing

**You can use:** sand, water, marbles, jar with lid, spoon

**1** Pour some sand into a jar. Add some marbles. Mix them with the sand. Has the sand changed? Have the marbles changed?

**2** Now add water. Mix again. You still have a mixture. None of the things has changed.

**3** Can you think of ways to separate this mixture? ■

123

In a mixture, molecules do not change. Mix sand and marbles. The sand stays the same. The marbles stay the same.

You can add water, too. You still have a mixture. The sand and the marbles do not change. The water does not change.

## Taking a Mixture Apart

Now suppose you mix sugar and water. Does the water change? It looks the same but it tastes sweet. Does the sugar change? You can't see the sugar but you can taste it. Do you think you have a mixture?

If you have a mixture, you can separate its parts. Try to separate the sugar and the water. Let the water evaporate. The water goes into the air but sugar stays behind. ■ You can separate sugar and water. The sugar does not change. Neither does the water. So adding sugar to water makes a mixture.

## Using a Filter

It is easy to separate a mixture of sand and marbles. You just pull out all the marbles. You can separate a mixture of sugar and water. You let the water evaporate—go into the air.

Now try this. How can you separate a mixture of sand and water? You could let the water evaporate but that takes a long time. There is a faster way.

You can use a filter to separate sand and water. ● Liquid water goes through the filter. Solid sand stays behind. With a filter you can take apart some mixtures. *ACTIVITY*

## *Separating*

**You can use:** jar, rubber band, paper towel, your sand and water mixture

1 Make a filter. Push the paper towel into the jar to make a kind of bag. This is the filter. Hold it in place with a rubber band.

2 Use the mixture you made for the activity on page 123. Take out all the marbles. Mix the sand and the water. ■

3 Pour the mixture slowly into the filter. ● Which goes through the filter, the sand or the water?

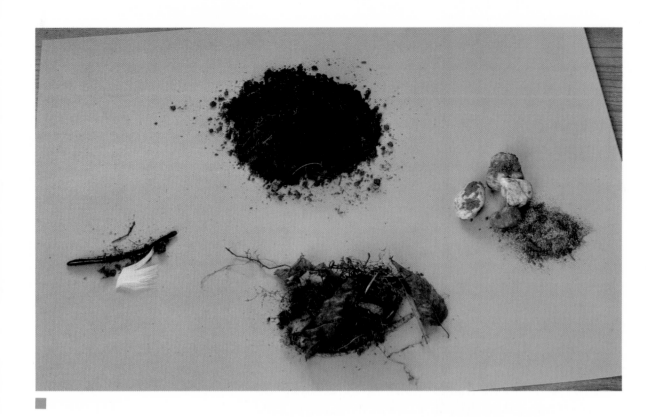

## Other Mixtures

You know salad is a mixture. Soil is a mixture, too. ■ Soil is made of small bits of rock and stems and seeds. It may have bits of tiny bones. Soil is a mixture of rock and parts of living things.

Some rocks are mixtures, too. You can see the different parts of these rocks. ● This rock is called snowflake lava. ▲ Why do you think that is a good name for this rock?

Are there other mixtures you can think of? Maybe some of your favorite foods are mixtures.

**127**

Write each sentence with the best ending.

1. In a mixture, the molecules
   all change    do not change

2. The parts of a mixture
   can be separated    cannot be separated

3. You can separate sand and water with a
   filter    jar

## YOU CAN DISCOVER

Put tap water in two glasses. Add a teaspoon of salt to one glass. ■ Stir. Which water is more like ocean water? Why?

Getting a haircut changes the way you look. ● Yet your hair doesn't really change, does it? It is just shorter than it was before. Cutting hair is one kind of change.

●

Cutting any piece of matter is the same kind of change. ▲

129

Cut a candle in half and you have two pieces of candle. ■ Both pieces are still made of candle wax. Each piece can still be a candle.

Suppose a candle burns. ● Soon you won't have a candle anymore. The candle wax will change to other substances. These substances go into the air.

Cutting the candle in pieces is one kind of change. It is a **physical change.** In a physical change molecules stay the same.

Burning is a different kind of change. It is a **chemical change.** In a chemical change molecules change. If you burn a piece of toast, you change some of the molecules of the bread. *ACTIVITY*

## Making Molecules Change

**You can use:** 2 slices of white bread, toaster, tongs

**1** Do this activity with the help of your teacher. Put one slice of white bread in the toaster.

**2** Let the slice get very, very dark. You may have to put the slice down two or three times. (*Use gloves or wooden tongs to pick up the hot toast.*)

**3** Look at the burned part of the toast. Compare it with the bread. ■ Do they look the same? Do they smell or taste the same?

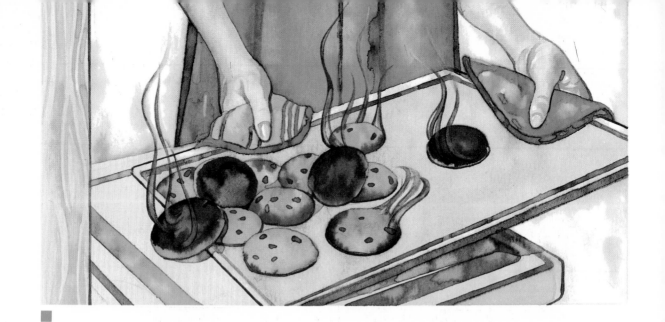

## Molecules Break Down

When toast burns, the black substance left behind is *carbon*. You may have seen this substance before. Was it on a batch of burned cookies perhaps? ■

If you burn sugar, you will see carbon, too. Burning is a chemical change. Sugar molecules break down and new substances are made. One substance, water, goes into the air. Carbon is left behind. ● It does not look like sugar. It does not taste like sugar. It isn't sugar.

If you just add sugar to water, you do not get carbon. The sugar molecules do not break down. They mix with the molecules of water. You can let the water evaporate. The sugar will be left behind. Dissolving sugar is a physical change.

Write each sentence with the best ending.

1. Tearing a piece of paper is a
   chemical change     physical change

2. Burning a piece of paper is a
   chemical change     physical change

3. In a physical change, molecules
   change     stay the same

4. In a chemical change, molecules
   change     stay the same

## YOU CAN DISCOVER

Suppose a bicycle is left outdoors on damp nights. In a few weeks you see reddish-brown spots on the bicycle. ▲ A new substance is forming. Do you know what the substance is?

## Three Jobs that Use Water

Off the truck they jump. They attach the hose to a hydrant. On goes the pump. In a great spray, the water rushes out. ■ The firefighters point the heavy hoses at the burning building.

Water is important in a firefighter's job. What other people use water in their jobs?

Did you think of hockey players? ● The water they use is frozen. On their sharp skates, they can move quickly on the slippery ice.

Dentists may use another form of water. They clean their tools with hot water vapor. ▲ Are you beginning to see how important water is in many different jobs?

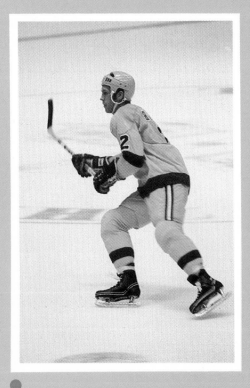

✓ All things are made of matter.

✓ Matter can be a solid, a liquid, or a gas. All of these forms of matter are made of molecules.

✓ Matter can change from one form to another. When matter changes form, nothing is lost or gained.

✓ A substance can change if its molecules change. When molecules change, a chemical change takes place. Burning is a chemical change.

✓ In a physical change, molecules stay the same. Making a mixture is a physical change. Melting is a physical change.

✓ The main ideas of this unit are:

**Matter is made up of molecules.**
**Matter can be changed.**

## A. CHOOSE THE BEST ANSWER.

1. The smallest part of something is a
   molecule    gas    liquid

2. Matter that has its own shape is a
   solid    liquid    gas

3. You find out about matter by using
   your senses    only your eyes
   only your hands

4. These molecules move more than any others.
   They are molecules of a
   solid    liquid    gas

5. Burning sugar is a
   chemical change    physical change

6. Dissolving sugar is a
   chemical change    physical change

## B. WHAT KIND OF CHANGE TAKES PLACE?

1. A glass window is broken.

2. Leaves burn in a fire.

3. You add sugar to water.

4. Ice cubes melt.

5. Gasoline burns in an engine.

# Find Out More

Ice can melt and become liquid water. Water can go into the air. It becomes water vapor. These changes take place slowly. How can you make the changes take place faster?

# Challenge Your Thinking

Peter wrote a secret message with lemon juice. We can't see the writing but his friend can. She holds the paper over a warm light bulb. ■ Does the lemon juice change? How? What kind of change is this?

# Energy on Planet Earth

You change as you grow. The street where you live changes. Perhaps there are more buildings than there were years ago.

The way people live and work changes, too. Could people travel by car 200 years ago? Could they light cities with electric lights? Could they make cloth by machine? Energy has made these changes possible. There is energy on Planet Earth. We have learned to use this energy in many ways.

At a circus or a state fair, you might get a big bright pinwheel. ■ In the wind, the pinwheel will spin.

Wind is air. It is air on the move. The wind makes the pinwheel spin. It takes **energy** to make things move. Ride your bicycle up a hill. ● Pull a wagon along the street. You need energy to make these things move. You get your energy from the foods you eat.

It takes energy to move the pinwheel, too. Where does that energy come from? The energy comes from wind—moving air.

## Using the Energy of Air

On a lazy summer day, the air is still. The trees are straight and tall. Not a leaf is moving. ▲  Now watch as the weather changes. The trees bend. The leaves toss about. ◆

The air isn't still anymore. It is moving. It is a wind. Wind has energy. The energy of the wind can move leaves. It can make a pinwheel spin.

People use the energy of the wind. Let's find out how.

In Clayton, New Mexico, there is a strange machine. ■ It is a windmill. The tall tower has two huge blades at the top. In the wind, the blades turn. Inside the windmill, wheels turn as the blades turn. The wheels turn machines that give out electric energy.

The windmill changes energy. It takes the energy from moving air. It changes it to electric energy. The electric energy goes to homes.

# The Energy of Water

Still water is like still air. It can't move leaves or trees. ● Moving water can, though. Moving air has energy. Moving water has energy, too. See how the energy of moving water moves this boat. ▲

The moving water of a river can also move rocks and soil. It can carry them over long distances. The faster the water moves, the more rocks and soil it can carry.

You can use the energy of moving water to make a pinwheel spin. *ACTIVITY*

●

▲

143

## Does Water Have Energy?

**You can use:** pinwheel, pitcher of water, jar

1 Hold the pinwheel over a jar of water. ■ Part of the wheel should be in the water. Does the wheel turn?

2 Now ask a friend to hold the wheel over an empty jar. Pour water on one edge of the wheel. ● Does the wheel turn? Does moving water have energy?

## Using the Energy of Water

In a flood, the energy of moving water can destroy houses or trees. Let's see how moving water can be safe to use.

This strong wall is a dam that holds back the water of a river. ■ Energy is stored in the still water.

Now gates in the dam open. The water rushes through pipes. The moving water has energy! It turns wheels. The wheels turn machines that give out electric energy.

Electric energy can work for you. ● Think of the ways you use electric energy.

Write each sentence. Then underline the ones where the energy of moving air or moving water is used.

1. A pile of leaves blows away.

2. Waves push shells on a beach.

3. A cloud moves across the sky.

4. Logs are carried along by a river.

5. Wind pushes against a brick wall.

## YOU CAN DISCOVER

Find pictures of things that move in the wind. ■ Find pictures of things that water can move. ● You may want to make a poster for your classroom.

# 2 ▶ Electric Energy at Work

Flip a switch. ▲ You can light up a dark room. You can wash clothes. You can listen to the radio. Electric energy makes these things happen.

You know that moving air has energy. So does moving water. Electric energy can move, too. It can flow along a special path. The flow of electric energy is called an **electric current.**

▲

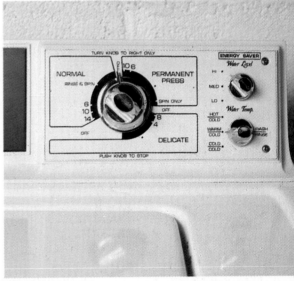

## Energy from a Dry Cell

You can get electric energy from a dry cell. Inside the dry cell are chemicals. ■ These chemicals have energy. You can change the chemical energy of the dry cell to electric energy. All you really need is a flashlight.

Inside the flashlight are dry cells. There is also a tiny light bulb. Suppose you turn on the flashlight. ● The bulb lights up. The chemical energy of the dry cells is changing to electric energy. Let's see how a flashlight works. *ACTIVITY*

148

## Making a Flashlight

**You can use:** 2 dry cells, covered wire, small light bulb, string

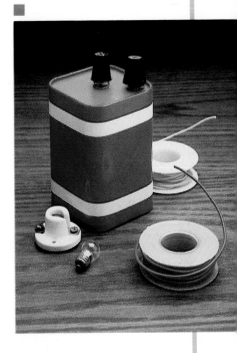

**1** Put a dry cell, wire, and bulb together. ■ Try to make the bulb light.

**2** In how many ways can you put these things together? Does every way make the bulb light? ●

**3** Now try two dry cells. How can you make the bulb light?

**4** Use a string in place of the wire. Does the bulb light?

## The Path of Energy

Trace the path of electric energy through a flashlight. ■ The bulb touches the top of one of the dry cells. The dry cells touch, too. The bottom of the second dry cell touches a metal spring. The spring touches a metal strip that travels along the flashlight. The other end of the metal strip touches the bulb.

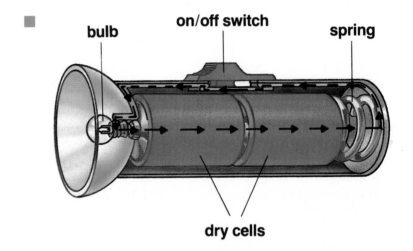

bulb          on/off switch          spring

dry cells

The path for electric energy must be complete. If not, the bulb will not light. Also, all the parts of the path must be metal.

Suppose you took away one of the parts of the path. Will the bulb light? No. The path is not complete.

Suppose you make a part of the path from string or from plastic. Will the bulb light? No. The path is not metal.

Write each sentence with the best ending.

**1.** Moving electric energy is called a
switch    current    wire

**2.** In a dry cell, the chemicals have
chemical energy    electric energy

**3.** For a current to flow, the path must be
broken    complete

**4.** For a current to flow, all parts of the path
must be
plastic    string    metal

## YOU CAN DISCOVER

Sometimes you can make electricity yourself. Here's how. Walk across a rug and touch a metal doorknob. Do you get a shock? That's electricity. Comb your hair. ● Does your hair stand out and crackle? That's electricity, too.

You go to visit a friend. At the door you ring the bell. Your friend hears the sound of the bell. ■ It is electric energy in the doorbell that makes the sound. Let's find out how.

Wrap some covered wire around an iron nail. Then attach the ends of the wire to a dry cell. Current flows through the wire. When the current flows, the nail becomes a magnet. We call it an **electromagnet.** What can an electromagnet do?

You can use the electromagnet to pick up paper clips. ●

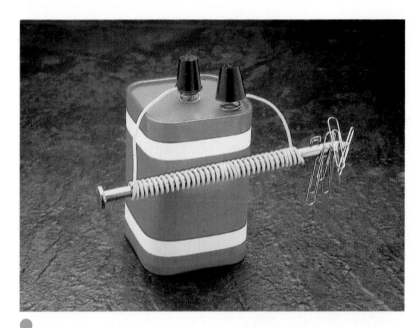

●

What happens if you unfasten one end of the wire? ▲ The current cannot flow. The nail stops being a magnet. Here is a magnet that can be turned on and off!

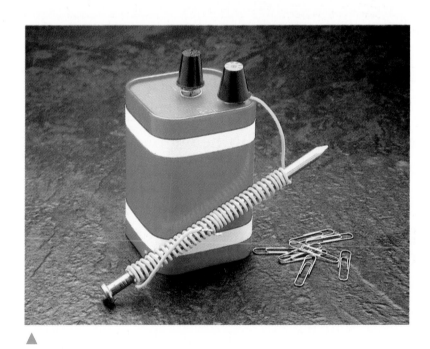

▲

## Electromagnets in Action

Electromagnets can move things. A big electromagnet can lift heavy pieces of iron and steel. ■ It can even lift a car!

A small electromagnet in a motor can turn blades. ● It can run an electric clock. It can make a fan spin. It can make a doorbell ring. How is sound made in a doorbell? *ACTIVITY*

## A Model of a Doorbell

**You can use:** clay flowerpot, iron nail, a nut or screw, covered wire, ruler, thread, dry cell

**1** Wrap some covered wire around a nail. Make the turns neat and close together. Leave two long pieces of wire at each end of the nail.

**2** Push the pieces of wire through the hole in the bottom of a flowerpot. Attach one end of the wire to one pole of the dry cell. ▪

**3** Put the pot upside down. Lay a ruler across the pot. With thread, hang the nut or screw from the ruler. Let it hang over the side of the pot.

**4** Now touch the second wire to the other pole of the dry cell. ● What happens? Try this a few times. Does your doorbell ring?

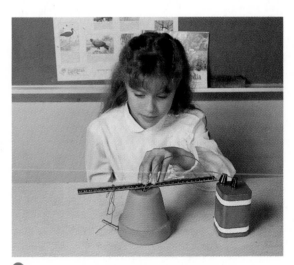

▪       ●

Inside a real doorbell are two coils of wire. ■ Press the button of the doorbell. Current flows through the coils. The coils become magnets. The magnets attract a piece of metal. The metal moves. It hits another object and makes a sound.

Stop pushing the button. The coils stop being magnets. The sound stops.

## Energy to Your Home

Think of all the ways you use electric energy. You need more electric energy than you can get from dry cells. How do you get the electric energy you need?

A machine called a **generator** makes the electric energy you need. A generator is really the opposite of an electromagnet. In an electromagnet, electric energy makes a magnet. In a generator, a magnet makes electric energy. Here's how.

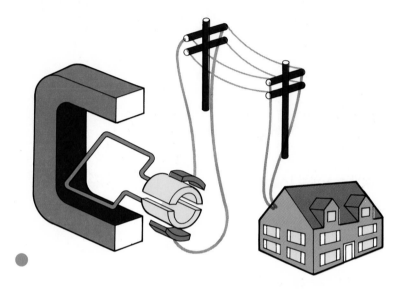

A coil of wire spins between the ends of a magnet. ● Then electric current flows through the wire!

From the generator, wires carry current to your home. Then you can use a toaster or a hair dryer. You can keep food cold.

## Using Energy Safely

We can learn about electric energy. We use dry cells. The energy they make is safe to use. The current in a house or in school is much stronger. It can be dangerous. You have to use it the right way.

**Here are some safety rules to remember.**

1. Have dry hands when you use electric appliances.

2. Never put a metal object into an electric appliance.

3. Don't plug too many appliances into one socket.

4. Don't put anything into a wall socket.

5. Don't use appliances that have torn or broken cords. Don't put cords where someone will trip over them.

## *Energy and Technology at Play*

What fun it is to look at the things in a toy store! But did you know that it can also be a lesson about energy and technology? Many toys need energy or technology to run.

This party favor gets energy from you. ■ When you blow into it, out it goes. What happens when you stop blowing?

This toy can walk all over. ● First you have to wind it. Inside the toy is a spring. When you wind the handle, the spring gets tighter and tighter. Then you let go. The spring starts to unwind and the toy marches along.

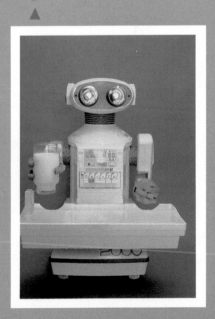

This robot walks. ▲ It can raise its arms and flash its eyes. It can answer the door. It can even talk to you! This robot can be programmed. Technology makes it work. Do you know any other toys that use technology?

159

Write each sentence with the best ending.

1. Electric energy can make a nail become a
   dry cell     magnet     generator

2. A magnet that can be turned on and off is an
   ordinary magnet     electromagnet

3. A magnet makes electric energy in
   an electromagnet
   a generator

## YOU CAN DISCOVER

Make an electromagnet. Use some covered
wire, an iron nail, and a dry cell. How many
paper clips can your electromagnet pick up? Then
make the magnet stronger. Use twice as many
turns of wire. ■ How many paper clips did you
pick up the second time?

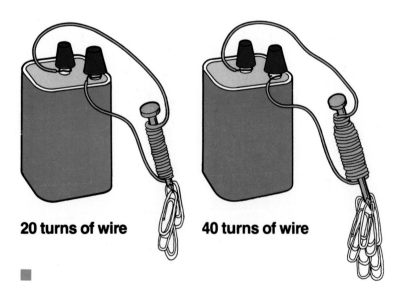

**20 turns of wire**     **40 turns of wire**

■

## 4 ▶ Energy of Fuels

Imagine being on a camping trip. At night in the forest it is quite dark. It is cold, too. You are far away from warm houses and electric lights. How do you keep warm? How do you see in the dark?

Someone collects wood to make a campfire. Near the fire it is light enough to see. ● Near the fire you can stay warm.

In the fire, the wood burns. As it burns, it changes. The burning wood is giving off energy. Wood is a **fuel.** There is chemical energy stored in fuel. When we burn the fuel, we get the energy. ■ You can feel the *heat* of the fire. You can see the *light* of the fire. Heat and light are two kinds of energy. We get heat and light from burning wood. We change the stored energy of the wood to the kinds of energy we can use.

How does the energy get into wood in the first place?

■

## Energy in Wood

A tree grows in sunlight. Energy from the Sun helps the tree grow. ● As the tree grows, it makes wood. Energy from the Sun is stored in the wood.

It takes years for energy to be stored in a tree. When we burn wood, energy changes quickly. It changes to heat and light. ▲ We need heat and light. So we use wood as fuel.

## We Need Energy

We need a lot of energy. We need energy to build houses and schools. Energy keeps us warm in the winter. It keeps us cool in the summer.

We get some of the energy we need from wood. To get wood, though, we have to cut down trees. ■ If we cut down all the trees, we would not have any forests. The homes of forest animals would be destroyed. Soil would be washed away by rain and blown away by wind. ● We can plant new trees, but it takes many years for them to grow. ▲

We cannot get all the energy we need from wood. We have to use other kinds of fuel as well.

Write each sentence with the best ending.

**1.** When we burn fuel, we get
   wood      energy

**2.** The energy stored in wood is
   chemical energy      electric energy

**3.** Heat and light are
   fuels      kinds of energy

**4.** Wood is a fuel. In a fuel there is
   stored energy      electric energy

**5.** When wood burns, the energy
   changes quickly      changes slowly

## YOU CAN DISCOVER

There may be fuels around your house. The
gas in a stove is a fuel. ◆    Is candle wax a fuel? ★
What other fuels can you find?

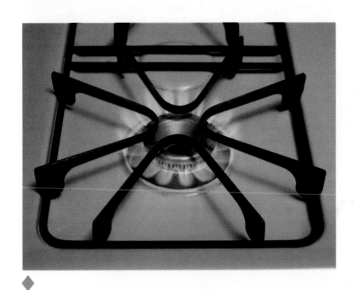

165

These are not ordinary rocks. ■ They are part of the treasure found in the Earth. Because they are hard to find, they are very valuable.

There are other treasures in the Earth, too. These treasures are more valuable than gold or silver. They are treasures that give us energy.

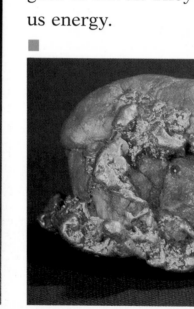

## A Rock That Burns

One of the treasures of Earth is **coal.** ● Coal is a rock. It is found below the surface of the Earth. Hundreds of years ago, people discovered that coal could burn. ▲ They burned coal to heat their homes. They used coal to run machines. Coal was even burned to run ships and trains. ◆

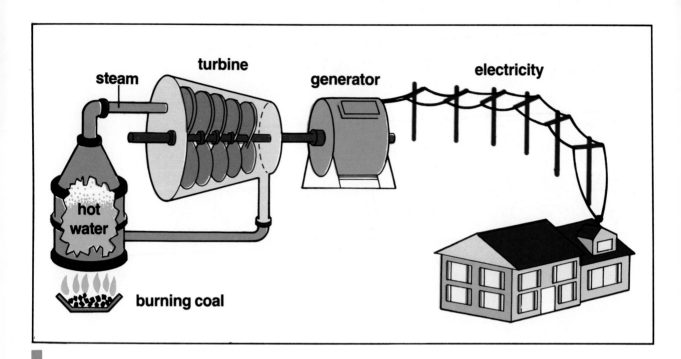

steam  turbine  generator  electricity

hot water

burning coal

Today many factories still use coal. We depend on these factories for many things. They give us steel for cars and cement for sidewalks. Bottles, cans, and paper come from factories, too.

How is the energy of coal used? ■ The coal can be burned. The heat from the burning coal boils water. Steam from the boiling water turns a generator. The generator makes electric energy. The chemical energy of coal is changed. It can become electrical energy.

## Where Coal Began

It is 250 million years ago. ● There are no people on Earth. There are forests of tall ferns. There are trees, too.

The air is hot and damp. Splash! A giant fern falls into the water. Crash! A strange tree falls on top of it. Leaves and trees lie in the water. More leaves and more trees are falling on them.

Sand and mud cover the plants. More plants fall. Layer upon layer builds up as time goes by.

Water flows in and makes a lake. Water and sand and mud press down on the buried layers.

Over thousands of years the layers change. The sand and mud change to rock. The layers of plants change to coal.

## Petroleum

The Hill family is going on a trip. They put their suitcases in the car. Away they go!

After a short time, the Hills stop to put gasoline in their car. ■ Gasoline is a fuel. Like wood and coal, gasoline can burn. As it burns, its energy can be used.

Gasoline comes from a thick, brown liquid called **petroleum.** Petroleum also gives us fuel for buses and trucks. It gives us fuel for ships and trains. From petroleum we get fuel to heat buildings. Petroleum is really a treasure. Where does the treasure come from?

Long, long ago, tiny plants and animals lived in the sea. When they died, they sank to the bottom. They piled up.

The dead plants and animals were covered by layers of sand, mud, and shells. Millions of years went by. The layers changed to rock.

The dead plants and animals changed, too. They became drops of petroleum inside layers of rock.

To get the petroleum, a well is drilled deep into the ground. ● Sometimes the ground is at the bottom of an ocean! ▲

●

▲

## Natural Gas

Sometimes there is **natural gas** above the petroleum. ■ Natural gas is a fuel. It is the fuel we use in a gas stove. We use it to cook food. We use it to heat homes.

Natural gas is made in the same way as petroleum. It is made from dead plants and animals that changed over millions of years.

Petroleum and natural gas have stored energy. It is energy that came from the Sun. The sunlight fell on the Earth millions of years ago.

Write each sentence with the best ending.

1. Coal is made from buried layers of
   plants     sand     rock

2. The stored energy of coal can be changed to
   chemical energy     electric energy

3. A fuel we get from petroleum is
   wood     coal     gasoline

4. Under the sea, dead plants and animals
   are buried. After millions of years, they form
   sand     petroleum     gasoline

5. Another fuel is made in the same way as
   petroleum. The fuel is
   natural gas     coal     wood

## YOU CAN DISCOVER

What kinds of rock can hold petroleum? Try
this and see. Take a few kinds of rock. Put a drop
of salad oil on each. ● Which rock holds the oil?

# Energy for the Future

The Earth has coal and petroleum and gas. It takes millions of years for these fuels to form. It takes only a short time to use up all their energy.

So people are looking for new ways to get energy. Let's look at what they have found.

## Solar Energy

This home is heated by a furnace, like many homes. ■ It is also heated by solar energy.

■

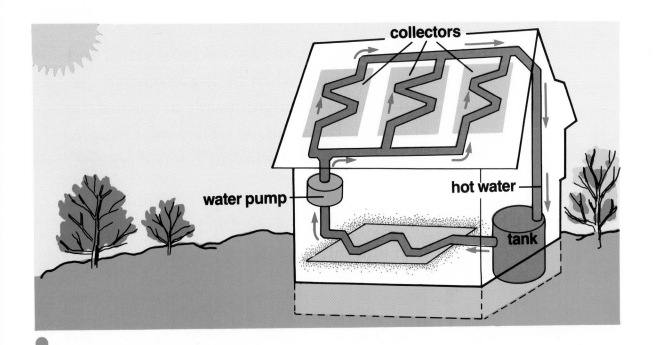

On the roof are solar energy collectors. Sunlight hits the collectors. The collectors turn the solar energy into heat. The heat warms water inside the collectors.

The hot water is sent to a large tank. It is stored in the tank. In this way, heat is stored in the tank.

What happens at night or when the Sun is behind clouds? The water in the tank can be used to warm the house. Or it can add to the heat from the furnace. Either way, fuel is saved.

We have always used solar energy. We use it to dry clothes on a line. ▲ We use it to grow plants. So solar energy isn't really new, is it?

▲

## Wind Energy

The electric energy for most cities and towns is made when fuels are burned. In some places, though, people are using the energy of the wind. ■ They are changing the energy of the wind to electric energy.

Windmills are new ways to make electric energy. Using the wind helps to save our coal and oil.

People have been using the energy of the wind for thousands of years. Wind makes huge ships sail across the water. ● The energy of the wind brought the ships of Christopher Columbus to America.

Wind also turned the blades in these old mills. ▲ As the blades turned, wheels inside the mills turned, too. ◆ The wheels ground grain into flour. ★ Is using the energy of the wind really new?

## Hot Springs

With a great whoosh, steam spurts from the ground! ■ Where does this steam come from? Deep underground, there are rocks that are very, very hot. Water near the rocks can get hot enough to boil. At a hot spring, boiling water and steam come to the surface of the Earth. The steam can be used to make electric energy.

So you see, the new ways to get energy aren't really new at all. They are new ways of looking at things.

■

## Learning to Save

Some of the ways to get energy are being used now. Many buildings use solar energy. Some towns may get part of their electric energy from a windmill or a waterfall.

Most of our energy still comes from burning fuels. We must save the fuels we have. Here are some things we can do.

1. Turn off lights or electric appliances when you are not using them.

2. Turn the heat down when no one is in the house or when everyone is in bed.

3. Don't leave outside doors open. Close doors and windows if an air conditioner is on. Turn off an air conditioner when no one is home.

4. Try showers instead of tub baths. Showers use half as much water. It takes a lot of energy to heat water.

5. Don't run the water all the while you are washing the dishes.

What are some ways you can think of to save energy?

## The Best of Old and New

Alvin Nez belongs to a Navajo Indian tribe. Some Navajos live like their ancestors did. They build houses of logs and earth called hogans.  They keep the hogans warm with a stove that burns wood or coal.

Alvin, some friends, and their teacher added a new idea to an old one. They built a hogan that uses solar energy.

Instead of logs and earth, they used bricks. One brick wall acts like a solar collector. During the day, the bricks get warm in the hot Arizona sun. At night, the bricks give off their heat. It passes to the air inside the hogan. The house stays warm in the chilly nights of the desert.

Sometimes adding a new twist to an old idea turns into a great idea. That's what Alvin Nez found when he helped build a solar hogan.

Write each sentence with the best ending.

1. Collectors change solar energy into
   fuel     heat     water

2. In a windmill, the energy of the wind changes to
   solar energy     electric energy

3. Underground steam can be used to make
   solar energy     electric energy

4. Most of our energy comes from
   wind     steam     burning fuel

## YOU CAN DISCOVER

In a dry cell, chemical energy changes to electric energy. What does a *solar cell* do? Where are solar cells used? ■

■

## Looking for Trouble

There is something wrong at the gas plant. But no one can find the trouble. They call in an engineer. ■

In this gas plant, natural gas is treated in a special way. Then it will be forced into an oil well to push up the oil.

The engineer has to study every step at the plant. ● After two weeks, the problem is found. One of the gas lines was blocked. The engineer goes off to another plant—looking for trouble!

# UNIT 5 REVIEW

✓ Energy has many forms. Moving air—wind—has energy. Moving water has energy. Energy can move things.

✓ We can change energy from one form to another. The chemical energy of a dry cell can be changed in a flashlight. It is changed to electric energy.

✓ A fuel has stored chemical energy. When the fuel is burned, the energy is changed. It is changed to light and heat.

✓ Wood is a fuel. Coal and petroleum are fuels, too. When a fuel burns, its stored energy changes to energy we can use.

✓ Coal and petroleum are found in the Earth. Scientists think they were made from living things millions of years ago. The energy of these fuels came from the Sun.

✓ The main idea of this unit is:

**Energy can be changed from one form to another.**

## A. TELL WHERE THE ENERGY COMES FROM.

1. A girl goes to school on roller skates.

2. A boy goes to school on a bus.

3. A flashlight is turned on.

4. Bread bakes in a gas oven.

5. A street sign blows down in a wind storm.

6. A waterwheel turns in a stream.

7. A doorbell rings.

## B. ANSWER THESE QUESTIONS.

1. We burn wood to get energy. How does wood get energy?

2. Write a story about energy. (Or draw pictures.) Show the ways we use energy every day. Show one special way.

3. How do scientists think petroleum was made?

## Find Out More

1. How do we get petroleum out of the ground? How do we know where it is in the first place?

**2.** Take a field trip right in your school. Find out what fuel is used to heat the school. Then have someone explain to the class how the school is heated.

**3.** In an electric current, particles move from one place to another. These particles are very small. They are much smaller than molecules. Find out what these particles are.

## Challenge Your Thinking

Imagine Planet Earth in two hundred years. In two thousand years. ■ Will we use the same kinds of energy? How will we heat our homes? How will we travel?

# Fitness to Live

Suppose animals could join the Olympic games. You are the judge. Which animals will win?

Will the kangaroo win the broad jump? Will a bird or an elephant lift something heavy? Which will travel faster over snow—a hare or a lizard? Will a turtle win a running race?

You know a lot about these animals before the games begin. The way the animals are built gives you a clue. Now you have a chance to find out more.

You will never find an octopus living in a tree or a camel on an iceberg. ■ You know the reason why. An animal must be **fit** to live in its environment. It must be able to get food. It must be safe from heat or cold. It must be safe from its enemies.

The parts of an animal's body help it to live in its environment. A bird's wings help it fly through the air. ● A tail and fins help a fish swim in water. ▲ Its gills help it breathe under water. The bird could not live under water. Yet a fish is at home there.

## Birds Get Food

This beak belongs to a macaw. ◆ The beak can crack open nuts and large seeds that are food for the macaw.

There are many kinds of birds. Not all birds eat seeds. Not all birds have a beak like the macaw either.

Look at the beak of a hummingbird. ★ How is it fitted for taking the liquid from deep inside a flower?

A blue heron doesn't eat seeds. It doesn't get liquid from a flower. With its beak, the heron catches fish and frogs. ☐

A pelican has a large beak with a pouch. The pouch can get very big. ■ The pouch looks like a fish net. What is the beak of a pelican fitted for?

## Insects Get Food

A mosquito's mouth is like a needle. The needle can stab the stem of a plant. ● Then the mosquito uses its mouth like a straw to take in liquid from the stem.

A grasshopper's mouth is fitted to chew on plants. It has tough, biting parts. ▲

## All Animals Are Fit to Find Food

Look closely at some other animals. You can find out how they are fitted to get food.

This crab uses coconuts for food. ♦ The crab climbs a palm tree and cuts down a coconut. Then the crab uses its strong front claws to break open the outer husk. Its job is not yet finished. The crab must also crack the hard inner shell. Then it can eat the sweet white coconut meat.

A tiger hunts other animals for food. ★ It has long, strong legs to run after an animal. It uses its strong claws and teeth to catch and eat the animal.

What does this animal eat? ■ Its name will give you a clue. It's a giant anteater.

The anteater uses its strong claws to open the nests of ants and termites. Its long, sticky tongue pokes into the tunnels of the nest. ● It picks up the insects it uses for food.

This whale is very big. ▲ It is much bigger than a large car. What do you think the whale uses for food?

This huge whale doesn't have teeth. So it can't chew large animals. Instead it has thin, bony plates that make a kind of strainer in its mouth. ◆

The huge whale opens its mouth. A lot of ocean water goes in. Along with the water go small ocean plants and animals. ★ The whale pushes the water out of its mouth. The tiny animals stay behind, caught in the strainer.

Do you think the whale is fitted to find food in its ocean environment? All animals are fitted to find food in their environment. They are fitted in different ways. *ACTIVITY*

## A Small Environment

**You can use:** a tree or an aquarium

**1** Pick a small environment. It may be a tree, an aquarium, or the soil under a rock. It may be at the edge of a pond. Look for animals that live in this environment. ■

**2** Now find things that might be food for the animals. You might see seeds or insects, roots or small plants.

**3** Draw pictures of the animals in their environment. ● How do they find and eat their food? Do they have long, sticky tongues? Strong beaks? Teeth? Claws?

What do these animal parts do?

## YOU CAN DISCOVER

Some animals can use "tools" to get their food. How does the sea otter open the shellfish it eats? ■

■

■

●

This desert is a hot, dry place. ■ It hardly ever rains here. Some plants grow in the desert, though. Some animals live here, too. In their burrows are snakes, lizards, and gerbils. During the heat of the day these animals will stay underground. Even on the hottest day, though, you can see a camel. ● Perhaps the camel is the animal best fitted for this environment.

Many of the camel's parts make it fit to live in the desert. Its bushy eyebrows help shield its eyes from the bright Sun. ▲ Long, curly eyelashes keep sand out of the camel's eyes. In a strong wind, the camel can close its nostrils. Then the flying sand won't get into the camel's nose.

Do you think the camel is fitted to live in the desert? Wait! There's more. The camel has wide pads on the bottom of its feet. ◆ The pads help the camel walk on the loose desert sand.

## A Camel Gets Food

A camel can eat many things. It eats wheat and oats. It eats desert plants, like dates. Sometimes plants may be hard to find. Then a camel may chew on a thorny cactus. ■ The lining of the camel's mouth is so thick that the thorns won't hurt it!

The camel has another part that makes it fit for the desert. Have you ever wondered why a camel has a hump? ● When a camel eats, some of the fats from its food are stored in the hump. When food in the desert is hard to find, the camel can live on the stored fat.

## Out in the Cold

You have probably seen pictures of bears in a forest. ▲   But have you ever seen a bear that can live in ice and snow? ◆   The Arctic is a cold, cold place. Yet it is the home of the polar bear. Seals live here, too. Whales swim in the icy waters.

How is the polar bear fit for the cold? Its thick, furry coat helps the polar bear stay warm. ★   Even the bottoms of its paws have fur. ☐   The fur helps the paws stay warm. It also keeps the bear from slipping on the ice.

▲

◆

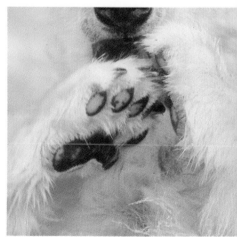

★   ☐

## A Polar Bear Gets Food

The bear uses seals for food. To catch a seal, the bear has to swim in the icy water. ■ The way the bear is made helps it to be a good swimmer. It has a smaller head and a longer neck than other bears. ● The body of a polar bear is thinner, too.

Do you see how a polar bear is fit to live in the cold?

## When the Weather Changes

Where you live, the summer may be very hot. Winter may be cold and snowy. What animals are fitted to live in an environment that changes?

The winter snow covers much of the grassland. But the bison can still stay warm. Their thick, shaggy coats help keep them warm. ▲ The bison can look for food under the snow.

▲

In spring, the bison have newborn calves. ■ There is plenty of tender grass for the young to eat. In the warm months, the bison shed their coats. ● The coats will grow back again before the next winter comes.

## Sleeping Through Winter

Heavy winter coats help make bison and polar bears fit for the cold. Not all animals grow heavy winter coats. Even so, they can protect themselves when the temperature goes down.

The tiny dormouse eats nuts and berries all summer and fall. In winter, food will be hard to find. Yet in winter the dormouse will not be looking for food. It will be asleep! ▲   It will sleep until spring comes.

Many bears sleep through the winter. In September, a bear will be fat from all the food it has eaten. It will look for a cave or a hollow tree to sleep in. ◆   Once in a while, a bear may open its eyes and look around. But it will not eat or leave its cave until April.

Other animals sleep all winter, too. Some frogs and turtles hide away until better weather comes. ★

## Animals That Travel

Have you ever seen a sky full of birds? ■ Where are all the birds going?

Every year, these Canada geese make a trip. In the fall they fly south to a warmer place. They will fly to a place where food is plentiful. They may lay their eggs there, too. ● When spring comes to the north, the geese will return there.

Do you live where winters are cold? Then you may know about another bird that flies south for the winter. ▲ When does the bird return?

Write each sentence with the best ending.

1. An animal that is fitted to live in the desert is a
   camel      polar bear      duck

2. To be fitted to live in the Arctic, a polar bear has
   whiskers      large ears      a thick coat

3. In winter, most bears
   stay active      sleep in caves

4. In winter, Canada geese
   fly south      stay in the north

## YOU CAN DISCOVER

Study a pet dog or cat. ◆      Pick one that has a thick coat. Does its coat get even thicker in winter?

◆

These small animals are called prairie dogs. ■ They are not dogs at all. They are really members of the ground squirrel family.

Many prairie dogs live together in a kind of town. They dig burrows deep in the ground. Each burrow has many rooms. ● One room is for sleeping. Another room is for food. The prairie dogs gather seeds, leaves, and roots of grass plants. They store away some of this food for the winter.

The prairie dogs watch for other animals that hunt them. They watch for coyotes. ▲ They watch for rattlesnakes. Hawks, eagles, and owls are enemies, too.

At a sign of danger, one prairie dog makes a loud whistling sound. All the prairie dogs run into the burrow! They are safe in their underground home.

▲

## Blending into the Background

Did you ever want to be invisible? You could be in a room and no one could see you. Of course, that can't happen.

Some animals can do the next best thing. They can hide so well that they almost disappear.

There is a butterfly on these leaves. ■ You will have to look closely to see it. The wings of the butterfly are folded. They are brown just like the leaves. They have the shape of the leaves, too.

▲

Watch what happens when the butterfly opens its wings. ● When is the butterfly safe from a hungry bird?

There is a bird in this picture. ▲ Can you find it? The bird is called a bittern. It makes its nest in the tall brown reeds.

The bittern has a long neck and a thin body. When it stands and stretches its neck, it looks like a reed!

The dead-leaf butterfly can hide in brown leaves. The bittern can hide in the tall reeds. These animals are safe from some of their enemies. Their shape and color help them to be safe.

## Other Ways to Be Safe

Some animals do not have the right shape or color to keep them safe. They may have something else though. Look at this porcupine. ■ When it is in danger, up go its quills. ● The quills are very sharp and can hurt an enemy.

Have you ever seen this furry black-and-white animal? ▲ Be careful if you do. The skunk doesn't have sharp quills. When it is scared, the skunk gives off a strong smell. Most of its enemies run away!

■ ●

▲

A zebra stops to drink water. ◆ It watches and listens for a hungry lion. A zebra doesn't have sharp quills to hurt a lion. It can't hide from a lion. A lion can see the bright black and white strips a long way off. To be safe, a zebra has to run—and run fast. ★

A zebra is fit to live in its environment. Could a polar bear find food here? Could it be safe from the hot Sun? No. Each animal is fitted to live in its environment. It is fitted to find food. It is safe from heat and cold. It is safe from its enemies.

★

## Animal Secrets

Where do birds fly when it gets cold? How often do bears need to eat? What animals sleep during the winter? Scientists are finding the answers to these questions by using modern technology.

Scientists put a kind of radio on an animal. The radio sends a signal, which tells the scientist where the animal is. Then, the scientist can watch the animal to study its behavior. Sometimes, satellites are used to find the animal.

By using this technology, scientists can study the places animals go. Also, they can learn what animals like to do, where they like to live, and how they get food.

Write each sentence with the best ending.

1. For food, prairie dogs gather
   grass plants        cactus plants

2. When they are in danger, prairie dogs
   change color        hide in burrows

3. When a bittern is in danger, it
   changes color        hides in brown reeds

## YOU CAN DISCOVER

This small animal is called an anole. ■ Is it green? Or is it brown? Or can it change color?

213

A monkey leaps from tree to tree. It can get a firm hold on a branch with its tail. ■ A juicy meal is in reach of its long arm. ● This monkey is fitted for its life in the forest. Being able to find food is an important part of fitness.

For animals to survive they must also reproduce. ▲ If monkeys did not reproduce, there would be no more monkeys. These animals would die out.

All animals make more of their own kind. The young animals must eat, grow, and be safe from harm. Are the young protected as they grow?

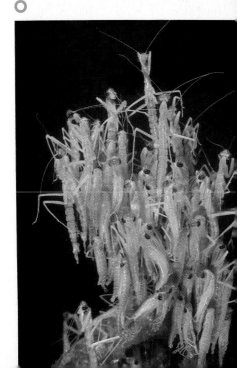

## Starting Out Alone

Inside the case are hundreds of eggs. ◆ The eggs were laid by a spider. The spider spun a silken case that protects the eggs.

In the spring the young spiders leave the case. ★ Each one spins a thin thread. The wind picks up the threads—and the spiders, too. Off they fly like tiny balloons on fine strings.

These young spiders are ready to start life on their own. No adult will care for them. Yet they can spin their own webs. They can find their own food.

Many animals start life this way. They survive on their own. Some snakes, lizards, and fish do not need the care of adults. □ Most insects don't either. ○

## Getting a Helping Hand

Other animals start life in a different way. They need the food their parents bring them. They need to be kept warm. They need to be kept safe. It will take time for them to learn to be on their own.

These baby birds will be helpless for weeks. Their eyes are still closed, but their mouths are open. ■ The adults will bring food back to the nest. Into the open mouths goes the food. ●

When the birds are strong enough, the flying lessons start. It only takes a few to get them into the air.

For young grebes the water of the lake is cold. It is dangerous, too. There are turtles and other animals that could harm them.

To keep the chicks safe, the mother carries them on her back. ▲   In a river in Africa, a young hippo wants a ride, too. ◆

An otter floats holding on to her young. ★ Soon she must search for food. So she wraps kelp around her baby. Now the young otter will not float away. ☐   It is safe until her return.

▲

◆

★

☐

217

## Learning at Play

A young bobcat plays in the snow. ■ It chases a passing mouse. The mouse gets away easily. ● The cat goes back to its game.

Bobcats spend a lot of time playing. It looks like fun to us. Yet for cats playing is very important.

For now young bobcats share the food their mother catches. In a few months they will have to find their own food. Playing a hunting game helps them. They learn the skills they need to hunt. They learn to defend themselves from enemies.

Many young animals learn by playing. ▲ In time the strongest or quickest young animal may become the leader of a herd. The lessons animals learn in play may last a lifetime.

Which animals need care when they are young?
Which do not?

otters

hippos

insects

snakes

## YOU CAN DISCOVER

These young seals still cannot find food on their own. ◆ They must get food from their parents. ★ Yet how can a parent find its young in such a crowd? (Hint: How do you recognize a friend on the telephone?)

◆ ★ **219**

## SCIENCE AND YOUR CAREER

## *Fitness Under the Sea*

The divers sink down into the clear water. They swim to the coral reef. A parrot fish peers into a face mask, then darts away. ● Well, it's time to go to work.

These people are scientists. Did you guess? The scientists are learning about the fitness of animals of the coral reef. So they travel to their undersea environment.

They learn what the animals use for food. They discover how they protect themselves from enemies. They watch to see if the environment of the coral reef changes.

So you see, the ocean is not such a strange place to find scientists after all.

# UNIT 6 REVIEW

✓ An animal must be fitted to live in its environment.

✓ The parts of an animal's body help it live in its environment.

✓ In different ways, all animals are fitted to find food.

✓ Animals must be safe from heat and cold.

✓ In different ways, animals can be safe from enemies.

✓ There are many kinds of environments on Earth. Each living thing must find what it needs in its environment.

✓ **Each kind of living thing is fitted to live in its own environment.**

## A. MATCH THE ANIMALS WITH THEIR PARTS.

1. polar bear        4. fish

2. camel             5. mosquito

3. pelican           6. whale

a.

b.

c.

d.
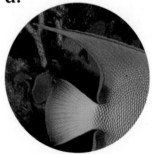

e.

f.
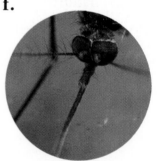

## B. ANSWER THESE QUESTIONS.

1. Pick an animal you have learned about. How is it fitted to live in its environment?

2. Suppose a camel lived in the Arctic. Could it find food? Could it be safe from the cold?

# Find Out More

1. Sometimes environments change. People can change them, too. What happens to animals then? Are any animals in danger today? ■

2. What animals live in a city environment? How do they get food? Can they be safe from enemies?

# Challenge Your Thinking

In a way, this animal has two lives. ● But it is not an amphibian. In the first part of its life, it walks on many legs. It eats leaves and other parts of plants. In the second part of its life, it has wings. Have you ever seen one flying? What do you call it?

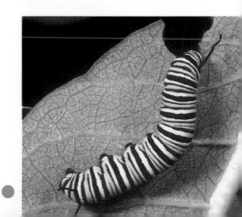

# People on Planet Earth

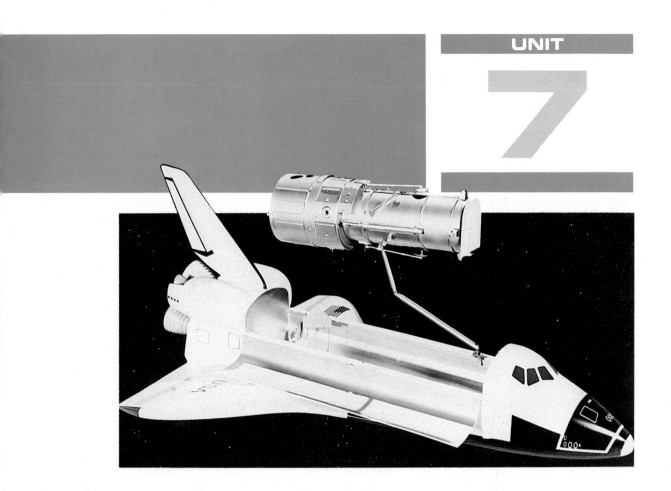

Why do people travel into space? Why do they explore the oceans? People explore, certainly, for adventure. Think how exciting it would be to land on another planet!

People explore for knowledge, too. They learn by exploring. You are an explorer, too. Every day you discover new things about your environment.

People are always exploring Planet Earth, our home. How do they use what they discover?

225

# 1 ▶ People Live in Different Places

How many girls and boys are in your class? How many are in your school? How many people live in your city or town?

These numbers may seem very large to you. Yet think of this. Over 4 billion people live on Planet Earth. If you began counting now and continued for two hundred years, you would never reach that number!

Many people on Planet Earth live in big cities. ■ You may be one of these people. Or you may live in a small town. ● Do you know someone who lives on a farm? ▲ Do you know anyone who lives on an island in the ocean? ◆

■

People can live in hot, dry deserts. They can live in cool places near the ocean. In fact, people can live in almost every environment on Earth.

## What People Need

Wherever people live, they learn how to get the things they need to live, grow, and keep healthy. We all need the same things. We need air to breathe, water to drink, and food to eat. We also need shelter for protection. We need a temperature that is not too warm or too cold. All over the world, people need these same things.  After all, we are very much alike, aren't we?

## People Get What They Need

Suppose you move far north, where winter is long and cold. Which house will you choose to live in? ● Why? What will you wear? ▲ Which clothing will keep you warmer?

Polar bears, remember, are fitted to live in a very cold environment. People are not. People have no fur or wool on their bodies. But they know how to use fur, leather, and wool from animals.

229

People learn to hunt and to catch fish. ■ On a grassy hillside some cattle can be raised. People grow wheat and fruit in the summer. They know how to store food for the long winter. ● They can buy food that other people have grown.

People design and build strong houses for shelter. They bring pipes to the house so they can have water. They design stoves and furnaces. They discover how to get heat and light from fuels. With the energy of steam or falling water, they produce electricity.

In these ways, people can change their environment. Then they can live where it is very cold. They can also live where it is very hot. They make changes by using their hands and some tools. What they are really doing is using their heads!

## A City of the Future

What would you need to live in space? Well, you would need many of the same things you need on Earth. First, you would have to build a place to live—a city, perhaps.

The Space Shuttle delivers your supplies. In space, you have no weight. Your supplies have no weight, either. So you can lift huge beams and move big loads. Your rocket car has mechanical hands that help you build a city in the sky. In a rocket backpack, you fly from one end of the city to the other.

Your city has a beautiful view. At night, you look through space and see Planet Earth. Your city has no storms. There are no earthquakes. Sounds fine, doesn't it? Yet you have some problems, too. There is no air or water. How can you change your space environment? How will you plan your future city in space?

Write each sentence with the best ending.

1. On Planet Earth, people live in
   one environment only
   almost every kind of environment

2. All people need air, water, food, and
   shelter from the environment
   a hot environment

3. People and polar bears both live in the Arctic.
   The living things fitted to live there are
   people      polar bears

## YOU CAN DISCOVER

When they hunt, Eskimos may live in a snowhouse. They make the house from blocks of hard-packed snow. ■

How can the Eskimos stay warm in this kind of house? Do you know the Eskimo name for the snowhouse?

■

# 2 ▶ Using Your Brain

Your body has many special parts. ●
You have a backbone. It helps you bend and
move. You have lungs. They help you take in
the air you need. You have senses. They help
you find out about your environment.

Perhaps the most special part of your
body is your brain. It helps you learn. When
you read, your eyes see words on the page.
It is your brain that really reads and
understands the words. It is your brain, too,
that helps you remember the words.

●

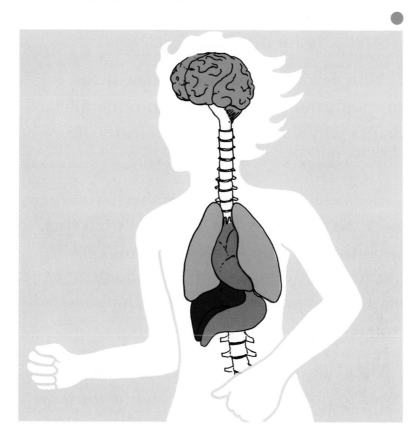

Suppose you are outdoors. ■ You feel drops of rain on your skin. It is your brain that gets the message from your sense of touch. Your brain sends you home for an umbrella and a raincoat.

Your brain is like a computer. It can store information. It helps you remember. That is why you don't have to learn the same thing over and over again.

Because your brain remembers, you know that water is wet. You don't have to touch the water to know that. You know that when it is snowing it is cold outside. You know that snow never falls on a hot summer day.

Because your brain remembers, it is easier to do a puzzle the second or third time. *ACTIVITY*

## *Picture Perfect*

**You can use:** pictures from magazines, scissors

**1** Make your own jigsaw puzzle. Pick a picture from a magazine. With your teacher's help, cut the picture into pieces. ■ (The pieces shouldn't be too big or too small.)

**2** Try to put the pieces together to form the picture. ●

**3** Now mix the pieces up and try again. Is it easier to do the puzzle the first time or the second time? How does your brain help you?

## Making Inventions

You use your brain in many other ways, too. You can make things you need. Take Rosa, for example. On a summer day, Rosa and her mother went for a walk. ■ Rosa saw some rocks that she wanted for her collection. She didn't have a bag or a box. So this is how she carried the rocks home. ● It was her invention!

People always **invent** things, make things for the first time. They invent tools to study the stars. They invent machines to help them build buildings. ▲

They invent heating systems to keep the buildings warm. To keep the buildings cool, they invent air conditioners. ◆ In this way, people can live in hot and cold environments. By inventing things, people can change the environment in many ways.

By inventing things, people can change the way we work. This machine is called a robot. ★ It can do some of the work a person can do. Some robots can do household chores. Others can put together the parts of a car.

People have new ideas all the time. Their ideas can even change the way we live. New ideas can make it easier to travel or to play. ■ They can even make it easier to see and to hear. ● People using their brains have made these things possible.

## Exploring Two Environments

Look at two special kinds of suits. ▲ Each of these suits is a wonderful invention. Each was made by many people working together.

Each suit has a supply of air. Each has temperature controls. Each has special boots and a helmet with a strong face plate to see through.

One suit has mechanical hands to pick up things from the ocean floor.

The other suit has a radio for sending and receiving messages in space.

Each suit is right for a person exploring a strange environment. Suppose you are an explorer. Where would you use each suit?

So you see, people can live in almost any kind of environment. We can invent things to change our environment. We have a remarkable brain.

## Robots

In today's world, robots are used to do many things. Because a robot has a computer for a brain, it can be *programmed,* or given a set of instructions, telling it what to do. A robot can do the same thing over and over again and never get tired of doing it. ■

One of the most important uses of a robot is to do jobs that might be harmful to people. One type of job is spray-painting parts in factories. Spray-paint might hurt a person's lungs, but it can't hurt a robot.

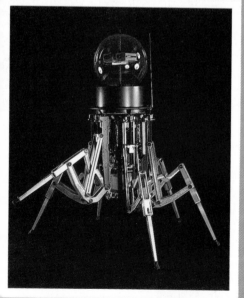

Some robots are used to study the ocean. Other robots, found in spacecraft, help collect material from space and send it back to Earth. ●

Scientists are studying robots to see if they can do other things. This robot, *Odex I,* can react to situations. ▲ In this photo, *Odex I* is raising its arm.

240

Write each sentence with the best ending.

1. A kind of computer your body has is your
   brain     eye     ear

2. Making something for the first time is called
   learning     remembering     inventing

3. People can live almost anywhere because they can
   make buildings cool     change their environment

## YOU CAN DISCOVER

How has the airplane changed the way people live? How has the airplane itself changed? ■

Your friend lives far away, in another town. Can you talk to your friend? You can call on the telephone, of course. ■ In a few moments, you are talking to each other. With the telephone, you can even talk to people across an ocean.

Things that people invent change the way we live. They make our work easier to do. ● They help us travel quickly. ▲ They keep us warm in cold environments.

Sometimes the inventions harm us though. Sometimes they harm us in ways we did not imagine beforehand.

## Changing the Air

This highway is crowded with cars. ◆ People are on their way to work. At the same time, though, something harmful is happening. The air near this highway is changing. It can sting your eyes. Some people may find it hard to breathe. ★ They may even become ill. Trees and plants may not grow well in this air. The air is becoming dirty, or **polluted.**

★

Cars burn gasoline. When fuels burn, remember, other substances are formed. Sometimes the gasoline does not burn completely though. Then some harmful substances are produced. These substances go into the air.

Cars are important to us. They help us travel. The car is an important invention. Yet the pollution it makes is a problem.

## Changing the Water

This factory makes paper. ■ The paper in your book may have come from a factory much like this one. The factory is important to us, isn't it?

■

Yet something harmful is happening there. Waste products from the factory pour into the river. The water is becoming polluted.

Oil, garbage, and other wastes are flowing into some of our rivers. Those rivers can become ugly. Others may even be dangerous. Living things may die in the dirty water.

## Keeping the Environment Safe

Today people are trying to protect the air and water we use. They make cars that burn fuel in a better way. Then the cars add fewer harmful substances to the air. People can filter out the particles from factory smoke. Then the particles can be used to make useful things. People can clean the water that carries factory wastes. Then the water will be safe for living things.

Here are ways you can help keep the environment safe. Put litter in a basket. ■ Litter makes a street or a park look ugly. It can attract flies and other animals. Help recycle paper, bottles, and cans. ● The paper, glass, and metal can be used over again.

BE A TREE SAVER

With an adult's help, make a garden in an empty lot. ▲  You will be helping to make your environment a nicer place. You will have fresh vegetables and flowers, too.

Help care for the trees and other plants on your street or near your school. In what other ways can you help?

# EXPLORING SCIENCE AND TECHNOLOGY

## All-Children's Playground

On a trip to Florida, you might visit many famous parks and sites. Some of these parks have rides, exhibits, and animals.

You might also visit another kind of park. It is called Turkey Lake Park. Turkey Lake Park has a special playground. It is a playground for both able-bodied and handicapped children. ■ It is called the All-Children's Playground.

The All-Children's Playground was built in five days by more than 5,000 able-bodied and handicapped volunteers. ● It had the support of the local government and businesses in the community.

The playground has a special design. There are no regular swings or slides. There are,

248

however, ramps and rubber surfaces for
wheelchairs. ▲ The ramps and surfaces make
it easier for all children to play together. ★ The
playground also has a submarine, an airplane,
a spaceship, and a treehouse.

## Environment and the Future

This book began with a trip through space. That trip isn't possible right now. Perhaps someday soon it may be. Someday soon, perhaps, people may live and work in space. They may live in space stations—on the Moon or in orbit around a planet.

In space we may find new sources of energy. We may find new ways to use the energy sources we have. In space we may find new materials or new ways to use the materials we have. ■

Now we live on the space station called Earth. We depend on its stores of air and water. We use electricity from its store of energy. We must use these stores wisely.

Suppose we move out into space. Then we will have a new environment to care for. We will have to use its stores wisely, too.

Write each sentence with the best ending.

**1.** Burning fuel in cars can make
   dirty air     clean air

**2.** The living things in a polluted river
   are safe     may die

**3.** Pollution changes the Earth
   in a bad way     in a good way

## YOU CAN DISCOVER

**1.** How much waste do people produce? Put all the paper and cans and bottles you use in a bag. ● After a week, weigh the bag.

**2.** We use water for cooking and washing. Is water a waste product? What happens to the water we use?

●

# SCIENCE AND YOUR CAREER

## Careers for the Future

When you are ready for a career, the world may be a very different place. After all, you could not have been an astronaut 50 years ago. In 1920 you would not have had a computer to keep track of information. Can you think of careers in the future that are not possible today?

Studying science is a good way to begin learning about your world. ■ You don't have to become a scientist to use what you learn. When you observe the color of a flower or the motion of a bird, you will be using science. When you fix a bicycle or bounce a basketball, you will be using science.

What you learn about the world will help you decide on a career. Science can help point the way.

✓ The Earth is home for many kinds of living things. It is our home, too.

✓ People can live in almost any kind of environment.

✓ People need air, food, water, and shelter.

✓ People use their brains to change the environment.

✓ Some changes—like pollution—are harmful.

✓ **We must help keep the Earth safe for all living things.**

## A. CHOOSE THE BEST ANSWER.

1. People all need the same things. They need air, water, food, and
   farms    cities    shelter

2. People can live almost anywhere because they
   are fitted to one environment
   can change the environment

3. The part of your body that helps you remember is your
   backbone    lung    brain

4. When people make inventions, like air conditioners, they
   change their environment
   keep their environment the same

5. Harmful substances form when
   people breathe
   gasoline is not burned completely

## B. ANSWER THESE QUESTIONS.

1. What do all people on Earth need?

2. Why can people live in different environments on Earth?

3. How do inventions help us? How can they harm us?

## Find Out More

1. Many Eskimos live in the northern part of Canada. How do they live today? ■ How did they live many years ago? ●

2. Find out if there is a recycling center in your city or town. If not, you may want to write a letter to city officials asking them to start one.

## Challenge Your Thinking

Suppose you could live in an underwater city. ▲ How would you get what you need to live? How would you get air? Food? Pure water?

# Glossary

Certain science words in your textbook may be new to you. These words are in dark print the first time they appear in the book. They are also listed in this glossary with their definitions and page numbers. The page numbers tell you where to find more information about the words.

Some of the science words have a pronunciation in parentheses. The pronunciation shows you how to say the word. The key below will help you pronounce some common word sounds.

| | | | |
|---|---|---|---|
| **a** | as in cat | **oh** | as in boat |
| **ay** | as in late | **oi** | as in toy |
| **air** | as in bear | **or** | as in born |
| **ah** | as in father | **oo** | as in pool |
| **aw** | as in ball | **ow** | as in cow |
| **e** | as in egg | **yoo** | as in use |
| **ee** | as in team | **u** or **uh** | as in sun |
| **i** | as in sit | | |
| **y** | as in ice | | |

**algae** (AL-jee), simple plants that do not have water tubes. Most grow in water. 85

**amphibian** (am-FIB-ee-un), an animal that usually has two stages in its life. During the first stage it breathes in water. During the second it breathes air. 47

**animal kingdom,** the group of living things that are like animals in all important ways, 35

**animals with jointed legs,** a group of animals whose legs bend at the joints. These animals have no backbone. Insects are in this group. 66

**animals with spiny skins,** a group of animals whose bodies have rough skin and sharp spines. These animals have no backbone. Starfish are in this group. 62

**astronaut** (AS-truh-naut), a person sent into space to study space and the bodies in it, 24

**backbone,** a chain of small bones along the back of certain animals, 57

**bird,** an animal that has feathers and lays eggs. Birds have backbones. Most birds can fly. 52

**carbon** (KAHR-bon), a substance that forms when sugar is burned, 132

**chemical** (KEM-ih-kul) **change,** any change in a substance that changes the molecules. Burning is a chemical change. 130

**chemical energy,** a kind of energy that is released by chemical change, as in a dry cell, 148

**chlorophyll** (KLOR-uh-fil), a substance in plants that gives the leaves and stems a green color. It helps green plants make food. 78

**class,** a group of living things that are like one another in important ways, 43

**coal,** a black or dark brown fuel that gives off heat when burned, 167

**computer,** a machine that can help people solve problems. A computer can also store information. 28

**cone,** the part of a pine tree where pollen and seeds are found. Pollen cones carry pollen. Seed cones carry seeds. A pine tree can reproduce from the seeds formed in its cones. 89

**crater,** a deep hole formed when space material hits the surface of another body in space. The Moon has many craters. 23

**dissolve** (di-ZOLV), to add a substance to a liquid so that it mixes completely with the liquid. Sugar dissolves in water. 132

**dry cell,** a device that changes chemical energy into electric energy, 148

**electric current,** the flow of electric energy through a wire or other metal path, 147

**electric energy,** a kind of energy that flows through wires, 142

**electromagnet** (i-lek-troh-MAG-nit), a coil of wire around a metal bar. When electricity flows through the wire, the bar becomes a magnet. 152

**energy** (EN-er-jee), the ability to move things, 140

**environment** (en-VY-run-munt), all things in and around the place where a plant or animal lives, 39

**equator** (i-KWAY-tur), a line that can be drawn around the Earth halfway between the North Pole and the South Pole, 9

**evaporate** (i-VAP-uh-rayt), to change from a liquid to a gas. Water evaporates and changes to water vapor. 119

**filter,** a device that can be used to separate certain mixtures. Sand and water can be separated by pouring the mixture through a paper filter. 125

**fish,** an animal that can live under water. Fish have gills to breathe under water. They have fins and a tail to steer themselves. Fish have backbones. Most fish lay eggs. 45

**fit,** to be able to live in an environment. Being able to find food is an important part of an animal's fitness. 188

**flower,** the part of certain plants in which the seeds are formed. Many plants have flowers. 86

**fuel** (FYOO-ul), anything that burns and gives heat energy. Coal is a fuel. 162

**fungi** (FUN-jy), a group of plants that do not have chlorophyll. They get their food from other living things. Molds and mushrooms are fungi. 93

**gas,** a form of matter. The molecules of a gas move about freely. A gas fills its container. 109

**generator,** a machine in which a magnet produces electric energy, 157

**hatch,** to break out of an egg. Birds, fish, and other animals hatch from eggs. 36

**hot spring,** a place in the Earth where boiling water and steam come to the surface. Hot springs may be new ways to get energy. 178

**insect,** a member of the group of animals with jointed legs. An insect has six legs and its body has three parts. An ant is an insect. 67

**invent,** to make something for the first time, 236

**liquid** (LIK-wid), a form of matter. A liquid changes shape. It takes the shape of its container. 108

**magnet,** an object that can attract materials made of iron and steel, 152

**mammal,** an animal that has a backbone and hair or fur. Its young develop inside the mother and are fed milk from the mother's body. 54

**matter,** what all things are made of. Matter takes up space. 104

**mixture** (MIKS-chur), two or more substances blended together without changing the molecules, 122

**mold,** one of the kinds of fungi. Mold has no chlorophyll. 92

**molecule** (MAWL-uh-kyool), the smallest part of a substance that acts like the substance, 112

**mollusk** (MAWL-usk), an animal with a soft body and usually with a hard shell. Clams are mollusks. 62

**moon,** a body in space that travels around a planet. The Earth has one moon. 14

**natural gas,** a gas that is found underground with petroleum. It is used as a fuel. 172

**nerve cord,** the bundle of nerves inside the backbone of an animal. It connects the brain to nerves in other parts of the body. 59

**orbit,** the path of a body in space as it travels around another body. The Earth is in an orbit around the Sun. The Moon is in an orbit around the Earth. 3

**ovule** (OH-vyool), the part within the pistil of a flower that becomes a seed, 88

**petroleum** (pet-ROH-lee-um), a thick, brown oily liquid that forms underground. It is used as a fuel. Gasoline and other fuels are made from it. 170

**physical** (FIZ-ih-kul) **change,** a change in which the molecules of a substance do not change. Dissolving sugar is a physical change. 130

**pistil** (PIS-til), the central part of a flower that holds the ovules. A pollen tube must grow down through the pistil before seeds can form. 88

**planet** (PLAN-it), one of several bodies in space that travel around the Sun. The Earth is a planet. 2

**plant kingdom,** the group of living things that are like plants in all important ways, 75

**pollen** (POL-en), grain of yellow powder formed on the stamen of a flower. It is needed for seeds to form. 88

**pollinate** (POL-ih-nayt), to transfer pollen from the stamen of a flower to the pistil. When flowers are pollinated, seeds form. 88

**pollute** (pol-LOOT), to make something dirty or unclean, 243

**reproduce** (ree-pruh-DOOS), to make more of the same kind. All living things reproduce. 37

**reptile,** an animal that breathes air. It has a backbone. It is covered with scales or hard plates. It lays eggs with leathery shells. 49

**ringed worm,** an animal with a soft body made up of sections. An earthworm is a member of this group. 64

**robot,** a machine that can do certain jobs, such as household chores, 237

**satellite** (SAT-ul-yt), a smaller body that travels in orbit around another body in space. The Moon is the Earth's satellite. 22

**sense,** a way through which the body learns about its environment. Hearing, touch, taste, smell, and sight are your senses. 109

**skeleton,** a system of bones that helps support an animal, 57

**solar** (SOH-ler) **cell,** a device that changes solar energy to electric energy, 181

**solar energy,** any of the energy that comes from the Sun, 9

**solar system,** the Sun and all the bodies that revolve around the Sun, 2

**solid,** a form of matter. A solid has a definite shape. 108

**spore,** a special part of some kinds of plants that can grow into a new plant. Ferns, mushrooms, and molds have spores. 90

**stamen** (STAY-mun), the part of a flower that produces the pollen, 88

**tadpole,** the young of a frog or salamander. Tadpoles live in water. They breathe through gills. 48

**water vapor** (VAY-per), molecules of water that move about separately as a gas. Water vapor is one of the gases in the air. It is invisible. 119

# Index

air: changing of, 243–44; as energy, 141–42; as matter, 109; pollution, 243–44

Aldrin, Edwin, 24

algae, 85

alligator, 49–51

amphibians, 47–48; eggs of, 47; environment, 47–48

animals: amphibians, 47–48; with backbones, 61; without backbones, 61–67; birds, 52–53, 189–90, 204, 209, 216–17; breathing, 45, 48, 49, 52, 54–55; environment, 39, 46–48, 50, 187–221; fish, 45–46; fitness to live, 187–221; food, 40, 51, 53, 189–93; fur, 55, 199, 201–02, 210; with jointed legs, 66–67; mammals, 54–55; mollusks, 62–63; reproduction, 36–37, 45, 47, 50, 52, 54–55, 62, 64, 66, 86–90, 94–95, 202, 214–17; reptiles, 49–51; ringed worms, 64; with spiny skins, 62; *see also specific animal*

anole, 213

ant, 67

anteater, 191

apple, 106

Armstrong, Neil, 24

astronauts, 24–26, 28

backbones, 57–60, 233; animals with, 57–60; animals without, 61–67

balloon, 109

battery, *see* dry cells

bears, 203; polar, 199–200

bees, 66

birds, 52–53, 189–90, 204, 209, 216–17; footprints of, 212

bison, 201–02

bittern, 209

blue heron, 189

bobcats, 218

bones, 127

book, 106

brain, 233–34; use of 236–38

breathing: animals, 45, 48, 49, 52, 54–55

brick, 109

burning: as chemical charge, 132; fuel, 161–63

burrows, 196, 206

butterfly, 209

cabbages, 122

camel, 54, 196–98

Canada geese, 204

candle, 130

carbon, 132

careers: future, 252; related to water, 134; in science, 252

carrots, 122

cat, 54

celery, 81, 122

changes: in energy, 140–83; in matter, 118–20, 129–32

chlorophyll, 78, 83, 90; plants without, 92–95

cities, 226

clam, 63

classes of animals, 43

Clayton, New Mexico, 142

coal: formation of, 168–69; as fuel, 167–68

coconuts, 191

Columbus, Christopher, 177

computers, 28, 240

cones: pollen, 89; seed, 89
crabs, 191
craters, 23

dam, 144
dentists, 134
desert, 196–97
dog, 54
doorbell, 152–56
dormouse, 203
dry cell, 148–50, 152

Earth, 5–6, 8–9; animals of, 35–71; day and night, 12; energy on, 8–9, 139–83; heated by Sun, 10–12; making changes on, 242–50; moon of, *see* Moon; people on, 225–53; population, 226; and Sun, 8–10
earthworm, 64, 65
eggs: of amphibians, 47; of animals with jointed legs, 66; of animals with spiny skins, 62; of birds, 52; of fish, 45; of owls, 36–37; of reptiles, 50; of ringed worms, 64
electric current, 147, 152–57
electric energy, 147–58; appliances, 158; in homes, 156–57, 230; and magnets, 152–56; using safely, 157–58
electromagnet, 152–56
elephant, 187
energy: of air, 141; changes in, 162–63, 168, 170, 172; conservation of, 246; electric, 147–58; of fuels, 161–72; in the future, 250; from hot springs, 178; on the move, 140; from natural gas, 172, 182; need for, 164; path of, 150; from petroleum, 170–71; at play, 159; saving, 179; solar, 9–10, 174–75; of wind, 142, 176–77
engineer, 182

environment, 39; of amphibians, 47–48; of birds, 52–53; changes in, 230, 242–50; exploration of, 238–40; of fish, 46; fitness to, 188–221; and the future, 250; keeping safe, 246–47; and plants, 92–93, 99; of reptiles, 50–51; in space, 250
exploration: in space, 2–6, 20–26, 231; for knowledge, 225

farms, 226
ferns, 90
filter, 125
fire fighters, 134
fish, 45–46, 220
fitness: of animals to environment, 188–221; to find food, 188–94, 198, 200, 201, 203; for heat and cold, 196–204; safety from enemies, 206–11; under the sea, 220; of young animals, 214–18
flashlight, 149–50
flounder, 46
flowering plants: 80–82, 86–88; *see also* plants
flowers: seeds, 86–88, 98; tubes in, 81
fly, 67
food: for animals, 40, 53, 189–93; mixtures, 122, 127; molecules in, 113; for people, 228, 230; for plants, 40, 78, 81, 83, 90, 92–93; from plants, 84, 86, 89
frog, 47–48, 203
fruits, 86, 88, 98
fuel: coal, 167–69; energy from, 161–72; natural gas, 172; petroleum, 170–71
fur, 55, 199, 201–02, 210, 229
fungi, 92–95
future, 250

gas: as form of matter, 109; from liquid, 119; molecules in, 120
gas, natural, *see* natural gas

gasoline, 170
generator, 157
gerbils, 196
gills, 45, 47
Grand Canyon, 4
grasshoppers, 66, 190
grebes, 216–17
green plants, *see* plants
greenhouse, 76, 98
grouping, 44
groups: of animals, 43–71; of plants, 43, 75–99

haircuts, 129
hare, 187
hearing, sense of, 109, 116
heat, 10–12, 162
heat trap, 11
hibernation, 202–03
hippos, 217
hockey players, 134
hogan, 180
houses, 180, 229–31
hummingbird, 189

Indians: Navajo, 180; Pueblo, 231
insects, 66–67; food for, 190
inventions, 236–40
iron, 108
islands, 226

jointed legs, animals with, 66–67
Jupiter, 15–16

kangaroo, 187
kelp, 84, 217
Kennedy Space Center, 30
kite, 106

leaves, 79, 82, 90; tubes in, 82

lemon juice, 115
leukemia: cure for, 84
light: from fire, 162
lion fish, 46
liquid: change to gas, 119; as form of matter, 108; from solid, 118
lizard, 49–50, 187, 196
lobsters, 66, 68

macaw, 189
machines, 236–37; electrical, 142, 145, 158
mammals, 54–55
marbles, 107–08, 123–25
Mars, 14–15; Viking spacecraft, 20
matter: 103–35; air as, 109; changing forms of, 118–20; chemical changes in, 130, 132; describing, 105; finding out about, 109–10; molecules in, 112–16; physical changes in, 129–30, 132; taking space, 106–07; three forms of, 108–09
Mercury, 3–4
mixture, 122–27; food as, 127; rocks, 127; salad, 122, 127; separation of parts, 124–26; soil, 127; using a filter, 125
molds, 92–95
molecules, 112–16; break down, 132; changes in, 129–32; movement, 119–20; in a solid, 118; in water, 120
mollusks, 62–63
monkeys, 214
Moon: craters on, 23; distance from Earth, 24; exploration, 24–26; orbit, 22; rotation 24; visitors on, 24–26
Moon Rover, 26
Mosquito, 190
moss, 75, 83, 90
mouse, 61, 218; footprint of, 212
museum, 103
mushrooms, 92–96

natural gas: formation of, 172; as fuel, 172, 182; plant (factory), 182; stored energy, 172

Navajo Indian, 180

neon (fish), 46

Neptune, 18

nerve cord, 59

Nez, Alvin, 180

octopus, 62

*Odex I,* 240

oil, 107–08

Olympic games, 187

orange juice, 108

orbit, 3

ostrich, 52

otter, 217

ovules, 88

owl, 36–37

park, 248–49

peach tree, 89

pelican, 190

people: brains of, 233–39; needs of, 228–30; places to live, 226–27

petroleum: formation of, 171; as fuel, 170; stored energy, 172

pigs, 54

Pioneer spacecraft, 21

pistil, 88

planets, 2–18; orbit, 3; travel to, 2, 20–27

plants: without chlorophyll, 92–95; color of, 76–78; flowering, 80–81, 86–88; food-making by, 40, 78, 83, 85; groups of, 43, 99; helping cure diseases, 84; reproduction, 37, 86–90, 94–95; with seeds, 86–89; without seeds, 90; with tubes, 81–82; without tubes, 83

plates: of reptiles, 49

Pluto, 18

polar bear, 199–200

pollen, 88–89; tube, 88

pollution: air, 243–44; water, 244–45

porcupines, 210

prairie dogs, 206–07

programming: robots, 240

rabbits, 55; footprint, 212

radio signals: for finding animals, 212

radish plant, 77–78

"Red Planet," *see* Mars

redwood tree, 75

reproduction: of amphibians, 47; of animals, 36–37, 214–17; of animals with jointed legs, 66, 215; of animals with spiny skins, 62; of birds, 52; of bison, 202; of fish, 45; of mammals, 54–55; of plants, 37, 86–90, 94–95; of reptiles, 50; of ringed worms, 64

reptiles, 49–51

ringed worms, 64

robot, 159, 237, 240

rocks, 127, 166, 236; in coal, 167–69; in petroleum, 171

roller skate, 106

rosy periwinkle, 84

safety: with electrical energy, 157–58; from enemies, 206–11

salamander, 47–48

sand, 125

satellite, 22, 212

Saturn, 17; Voyager spacecraft, 21

scales: of fish, 45; of reptiles, 49

science; careers in, 252

seal, 54, 200

seeds: in a flower, 89; without flowers, 89; how made, 87; plants with, 86–89; plants without, 90, in soil, 127 senses, 109, 233; smell, 115; touch, 234

sight, sense of, 109

skeleton, 57, 66

skunk, 210

smell, sense of, 109, 115

smoke detector, 116

snails, 63

snakes, 49–50, 196, 215

snowflake lava, 127

soil, 14, 64, 127

solar cell, 181

solar energy, 9–10, 174–75, 180

solar system, 2–18

solids: change to liquid, 118; as form of matter, 108

space: in future, 250; life in, 231; suit, 238–39; travel through, 2, 20–26, 231

Space Shuttle, 231

space station, 27

spacecraft: Moon Rover, 26; Pioneer, 21; Viking, 20; Voyager, 21

spaceship, 2

spider, 67, 215

spiny skins, animals with, 62

spores, 90, 94–96

springs, hot, 178

stamen, 88

stems, 127

sugar: dissolving of, 132; in mixture, 124; molecules in, 112–13, 132

Sun, 2; energy from, 9–10, 163, 174–75, 180

sunlight, 78

supermarket, 28, 35

sweater, 106


taste, sense of, 109

technology, 28, 68, 84, 116, 159, 180, 212, 231, 240, 248–49

tiger, 191

toast, 131–32

tomatoes, 122

touch, sense of, 109, 234

towns, 226

toys: and energy, 159

travel: to Moon, 24–26; types of, 1, 2

tubes: in plants, 81, 82

Turkey Lake Park, 248–49

turtles, 203


Uranus, 18


veins, 82

Venus, 4–5; Pioneer spacecraft, 21

Viking spacecraft, 20

vinegar, 115

Voyager spacecraft, 21


walrus, 39

water: animals that live in, 45–48; change to vapor, 119–20; as energy, 143–45, 178; jobs that use, 134; molecules in, 112, 114, 120; needed by plants, 78, 81, 83

water vapor, 119–20

watermelon, 86

whale, 54–55, 192–93

wind: energy from, 141–42, 176–77

windmill, 142, 176–77

wood, 108; energy in, 163; as fuel, 161–64

worms: earthworms, 65; ringed, 64


yeast, 101


zebra, 211

zoo, 70

zookeeper, 70

McCoy/Rainbow, (tc) Greg Edwards/International Stock Photo, (bl) Ken Lewis/Earth Scenes, (br) Breck P. Kent/Earth Scenes; **80**(both), **81**(both), **82**(both), Martin Bough/Corporate Studios Communications; **83,** Lowell Georgia/Photo Researchers; **84**(t), L. Mellichamp/Visuals Unlimited, (b) D. Puleston/Photo Researchers; **85,** Charlie Ott/Photo Researchers; **86**(t), Barry L. Runk/Grant Heilman, (c, bl, br), Grant Heilman; **87**(both), Martin Bough/Corporate Studios Communications; **89**(t), Zig Leszczynski/Animals, Animals, (ct, cb) Robert A. Ross/E.R. Deggnger, (bl) Virginia P. Weinland/Photo Researchers, (bc) John Colwell/Grant Heiman, (br) Martin Bough/Corporate Studios Communications; **90,** Manuel Rodriguez; **91,** HBJ; **92**(l), S. Ronnels/Grant Heilman, (r) Ken Highfill/Photo Researchers; **93,** W. H. Hodge/Peter Arnold; **94,** W. H. Hodge/Peter Arnold; **96**(both), Martin Bough/Corporate Studios Communications; **98**(t), Peter B. Kaplan/Photo Researchers, (b) A. W. Ambler/Photo Researchers; **101,** HBJ;

**UNIT 4: 102**(l), Sal Maimone/Shostal Assoc., (tr) The Smithsonian/Chip Clark, (br) Kent & Donna Bannen/Photo Researchers; **103**(t), Coco McCoy/Rainbow, (b) Bill Weems/Woodfin Camp & Assoc.; **105**(all), HBJ; **106**(t), HBJ, (cl, cr, bl, br), Martin Bough/Corporate Studios Communications; **107**(all), Martin Bough/Corporate Studios Comunications; **108**(t), Mark Antman/Image Works, (c) Grant Heilman, (bl, br) Martin Bough/Corporate Studios Communications; **109**(both), **114, 116, 117,** Martin Bough/Corporate Studios Communications; **119**(t, c,) HBJ, (b) Phil & Loretta Hermann/Tom Stack & Assoc.; **120**(t), Ruth Dixon, (b) Martin Bough/Corporate Studios Communications; **122**(both), **123, 124**(all), Martin Bough/Corporate Studios Communications; **125,** HBJ; **126**(both), Martin Bough/Corporate Studios Communications; **127**(t, b), HBJ, (ct) Russ Kinne/Photo Researchers, (cb) A. W. Ambler/National Audubon Society/Photo Researchers; **128**(both), HBJ; **129**(l), HBJ, (c) Dan McCoy/Rainbow, (r) Martin Bough/Corporate Studios Communications; **130**(both), **131, 132**(both), **133**(both), Martin Bough/Corporate Studios Communications; **134**(tl), George E. Jones III/Photo Researchers, (tr) Tod Friedman Photography/Sports Photo File, (b) Martin Bough/Corporate Studios Communications; **135**(t), Barry L. Runk/Grant Heilman, (b) H. Gritscher/Peter Arnold;

**UNIT 5: 138**(l), Mike Mitchell/Photo Researchers, (br) Carl Purcell/FPG; **139**(t), John Zoiner/International Stock Photography (c) Culver, (b) Granger; **140**(l), Dan McCoy/Rainbow, (r) Martin Bough/Corporate Studios Communications; **141**(l), Taurus, (r) C. C. Lockwood/Earth Scenes; **142,** Mark Antman/Stock, Boston; **143**(l), S. Zeiberg/Taurus, (r) Gerald A. Corsil/Tom Stack & Assoc.; **144**(both), HBJ; **145**(t), Bill W. Marsh/Photo Researchers, (c) Randy Matusow, (b) Martin Bough/Corporate Studios Communications; **146**(l), Kachaturian/International Stock Photography, (r) H. Armstrong Roberts; **147**(all), **148, 149**(both), **153**(both), Martin Bough/Corporate Studios Communications; **154**(tl, b), Randy Matusow, (tr) E. R. Deggginger; **155**(both), **156,** Martin Bough/Corporate Studios Communications; **159**(tl, tr), Martin Bough/Corporate Studios Communications, (b) Bill Foley/Time Magazine; **162,** Martin Bough/Corporate Studios Communications; **163,** Grant Heilman; **164**(t), Earl Roberge/Photo Researchers, (c) Roy Hankey/Photo Researchers, (bl) Frank Siteman/Stock, Boston; **165**(l), Martin Bough/Corporate Studios Communications, (r) HBJ/Kogler; **166**(tl, tr), Breck P. Kent/Earth Scenes, (b) Breck P. Kent/The Smithsonian Institution,Earth Scenes; **167**(t), Harvey Lloyd/Peter Arnold, (c, b), Culver; **171**(l), Jeremy Ross/Photo Researchers, (r) Earl Roberge/Photo Researchers; **173,** Martin Bough/Corporate Studios Communications; **174,** Hank Morgan; **175,** Linda Moore/Rainbow; **176**(l), Mark Antman/Stock, Boston, (r) Holt Confer/Grant Heilman; **177**(l), Thomas Zimmerman/FPG, (tr, b) Hank Morgan/Rainbow, (cr) Claire Taplin/Taurus; **178,** Neff/National Audubon Society/Photo Researchers; **180**(tl), Don Getsug/Photo Researchers, (tr, b) Richard C. Birky; **181**(both), HBJ; **182**(both), J. Alex Langley/DPI; **183**(t), Dan McCoy/Rainbow, (c) Bill Foley/Time Magazine, (b) Hank Morgan/Rainbow;

**UNIT 6: 186**(l), E. R. Degginger, (tr) Georgio Gualco/Bruce Coleman, (br) Jen & Des Bartlett/Bruce Coleman; **187**(t), Laura Riley/Bruce Coleman, (b) Claude Pissavini/Jacana, Image Bank; **188**(l), Stephen Dalton/Photo Researchers, (r) Dave Woodward/Taurus; **189**(t) George Holton/Photo Researchers, (bl), Walter E. Harvey/Photo Researchers, (br) Patti Murray/Animals, Animals; **190**(tl), E. R. Degginger, (tr) Tom Bledsoe/Photo Researchers, (b) Syd Greenberg/Photo Researchers; **191**(both), Zig Leszczynski/Animals, Anials; **192**(tl), Francisco Erize/Bruce Coleman, (tr) Joseph Van Warmer/Bruce Coleman, (b) Bruce M. Wellman/Tom Stack & Assoc.; **193**(l), Dr. Charles R. Belinky/Photo Researchers, (r) George Whitely/Photo Researchers; **194,** Martin Bough/Corporate Studios Communications; **195**(tl), Bob White/Animals, Animals, (tr) S. J. Kraseman/Peter Arnold, (cl) Ruth Dixon, (cr) Zig Leszczynski/Animals, Animals, (b) Jeff Foott/Bruce Coleman; **196**(l), George Geister/Photo Researchers, (r) Mickey Gibson/Animals, Animals; **197**(l), Jack Wilburn/Animals, Animals, (r) Marion Austerman/Animals, Animals, (b) Ruth Dixon; **198**(l), J. C. Stevenson/Animals, Animals, (r) Ken Stepnel/Bruce Coleman; **199**(l), R. Hamilton Smith/Photo Library, (tr) James K. Morgan/Photo Researchers, (cr) ProPix/Monkmeyer, (br) S. J. Kraseman/Photo Researchers; **200,** E. R. Degginger/Animals, Animals; **201,** Leonard Lee Rue III/Bruce Coleman; **202**(t), S. J. Kraseman/Photo Researchers, (b) Norman Tomalin/Bruce Coleman; **203**(t), Stouffer Productions/Animals, Animals, (bl) Jane Burton/Bruce Coleman, (br) Runk/Schoenberger/Grant Heilman; **204**(t), Helen Williams/Photo Researchers, (bl), John Serrao/Photo Researchers, (br) Gregory K. Scott/Photo Researchers; **206,** Tom McHugh/Photo Researchers; **207,** Leonard Lee Rue III/Photo Researchers; **208**(both), Breck P. Kent/Animals, Animals; **209,** Robert A. Ashworth/Photo Researchers; **210**(tl), Cosmos Blank/National Audubon Society, Photo Researchers, (tr) Harry Engels/Photo Researchers, (b) Leonard Lee Rue III/Photo Researchers; **211**(t), Russ Kinne/Photo Researchers, (b) Mitch Reardon/Photo Researchers; **212**(both), Larry B. Jennings/Photo Researchers; **213**(l), Robert C. Hermes/Photo Researchers, (r) Ken Brate/Photo Researchers; **214**(t), L. & D. Klein/Photo Researchers, (bl) F. Gohier/Photo Researchers, (br) Eric Crichton/Bruce Coleman; **215**(tl), Edmund R. Taylor/DPI, (tr) Robert W. Mitchell/Animals, Animals, (c) Zig Leszczynski/Animals, Animals, (b) Raymond A. Mendez/Animals, Animals; **216**(l), Gray W. Griffin/Animals, Animals, (r) Michael Habicht/Animals, Animals; **217**(tl), Bob & Clara Calhoun/Bruce Coleman, (tr) Herbert Levant/Photo Researchers, (bl) The Store Flower Studio/DPI, (br) Jeff Foott/Bruce Coleman; **218**(tl, tr, c), Leonard Lee Rue III/Animals, Animals, (b) G. L. Kooyman/Animals, Animals; **219**(tl), Herb Levant/Photo Researchers, (tc) Raymond A. Mendez/Animals, Animals, (tr) Jeff Foott/Bruce Coleman, (trb) Zig Leszczynski/Animals, Animals, (bl) John S. Flannery/Bruce Coleman, (br) Tom McHugh/Photo Researchers; **220**(t), Jim Beck/Animals, Animals, (b) Carl Roessler/Photo Researchers; **221**(t), Michael L. Smith/Photo Researchers, (c) Russ Kinne/Photo Researchers, (bl) Jeff Foott/Bruce Coleman, (br) Leonard Lee Rue III/Photo Researchers; **222**(tl), Tom Bledsoe/Photo Researchers, (tc) Dr. Charles R. Belinky/Photo Researchers, (tr) J. C. Stevenson/Animals, Animals, (bl) Dave Woodward/Taurus, (bc) S. J. Kraseman/Peter Arnold, (br) E. R. Degginger; **223**(tl, tr), Tom McHugh/Photo Researchers, (b) Breck P. Kent/Animals, Animals;

**UNIT 7: 224**(l), Del Mulkey/Photo Researchers, (tr) Rod Catanach/Woods Hole Oceanographic Institution, (br) David Muench/H. Armstrong Roberts; **225**(t), NASA, (b) Joe Monroe/Photo Researchers; **226,** George Hall/Woodfin Camp & Assoc.; **227**(t), Peter Miller/Photo Researchers, (bl) Earl Roberge/Photo Researchers, (br) Seraillier/Photo Researchers; **228**(tl), Bob Hahn/Taurus, (tr) Ginger Chih/Peter Arnold, (b) Malcolm S. Kirk/Peter Arnold; **229**(t), Helene Slavens/Peter Arnold, (c), Michael & Barbara Reed/Earth Scenes, (b both) HBJ; **230**(l), Dan Gueravich/Photo Researchers, (r) Porterfield-Chickering/Photo Researchers; **232,** Clyde H. Smith/Peter Arnold; **235**(r), HBJ; **237**(t), Martin Bough/Corporate Studios Communications, (bl) Donald Deitz/Stock, Boston, (br) Saito/PPS, Photo Researchers; **238**(t), Chris Brown/Stock, Boston, (b) Cary Wolinsky/Stock, Boston; **239**(l), NASA, (r) H. Steve Lissau/H. Armstrong Roberts; **240**(tl), NASA, (tr) Tom McHugh/Photo Researchers, (b) Malcolm S. Kirk/Peter Arnold; **241**(tl), J. W. Cella/Photo Researchers, (tr) Dan Gueravich/Photo Researchers, (b) Tom Gibson/Photo Researchers; **242**(t), Robert A. Clark, Jr./Photo Researchers, (b) Riviere/Rapho, Photo Researchers; **243**(t), Thomas Braise/Stock Market, (b) Owen Franken/Stock, Boston; **244,** Calvin Larson/Photo Researchers; **245,** Grant Heilman; **246,** HBJ; **247**(t), Mini Forsyth/Monkmeyer, (b) Richard Choy/Peter Arnold; **248**(l), Steven Dampier/City of Orlando, Fl., (r) HBJ; **249**(all) HBJ; **250,** NASA; **251,** Martin Bough/Corporate Studios Communications; **252**(t, bl), HBJ/Kogler, (br) Phoebe Dunn/DPI; **253**(t), George Hall/Woodfin Camp & Assoc., (bl) Richard Choy/Peter Arnold, (br) Saito/PPS, Photo Researchers; **255**(t, c), Jim Carter/Photo Researchers, (b) Marcella Bertinetti/Photo Researchers.